This Journal Belongs To

Year

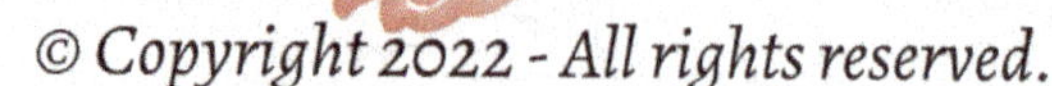

Dedication

Dedicated to the awesome lady holding this journal now.

I send you my love wherever in the world you are.

I want you to know you are amazing inside out.

You are a beautiful soul. You are stronger than you know.

You are unique. You are loved and You are enough!

Embrace Yourself!

Embrace and fall in love with life!

May lots of love, happiness, peace, joy, good fortune, and good health come your way and fill your life.

Wishing you beautiful days ahead!

Florance.

How to use this Journal.

It is proven that journaling practice can improve our mood, well-being, sleep, immune function, and emotional health while lowering levels of stress, anxiety, and blood pressure.

It is unlikely that you will get hold of this journal exactly on the 1st of January. You don't have to wait for New Year's dawn to start journaling. Start on whichever day of the year you got this journal and then follow through for the next 364 days.

Each journaling page starts with a carefully selected 'quote for the day'. You can jot down up to three things you feel grateful for in that moment - what do you appreciate most about your life right now? You can then add goals and dreams dear to your heart. You can also write your affirmation for the day, which is a very powerful activity in navigating towards or sustaining your happiness, peace, and ideal life. I have shared a list of my favorite affirmations in this book.

Feel free to then pen down your thoughts and feelings for the day. Write down whatever comes to your mind.

It can be helpful to set aside five to ten minutes in the day that you can dedicate to journaling. I usually aim to journal before starting my day. Find a time that works for you. Stick to that time as much as you can but remember not to be too harsh on yourself if you have missed a day or if you can't journal at the same time every day. Life happens! Celebrate and enjoy the pages you have written!

Journaling is a beautiful experience, it is so satisfying and brings a sense of calm and relaxation. It helps you to think, imagine, plan, remember, rant, discover, dream, feel gratitude, relax, unwind and slow down. When practiced regularly, it can be transformational.

I hope you love and enjoy this journal.

Much Love,

Florance

My Favorite Affirmations

- My body is beautiful, strong, healthy, and capable.
- I align with peace, good health, harmony, and abundance.
- I am at peace with who I am and where I am in life.
- All is well.
- I am loveable and valuable.
- I am beautiful inside out.
- I love my life, and I am grateful for this precious life.
- I am in charge of how I feel, and today I choose happiness.
- I choose positive, uplifting, and happy thoughts.
- I am kind, I am peaceful, I am happy and I am enough.
- I am worthy of all the good things in life.
- I live a life of happiness and gratitude.
- My success is inevitable.
- I live an abundant life.
- My dreams are coming true.
- I am grateful for everything I have and everything I receive.
- Today will be a good day.
- Everything I desire is already on its way to me.
- I have more than enough.
- My income is always increasing.
- I am capable of prosperity, success, and wealth

My Top Ten Goals
For This Year

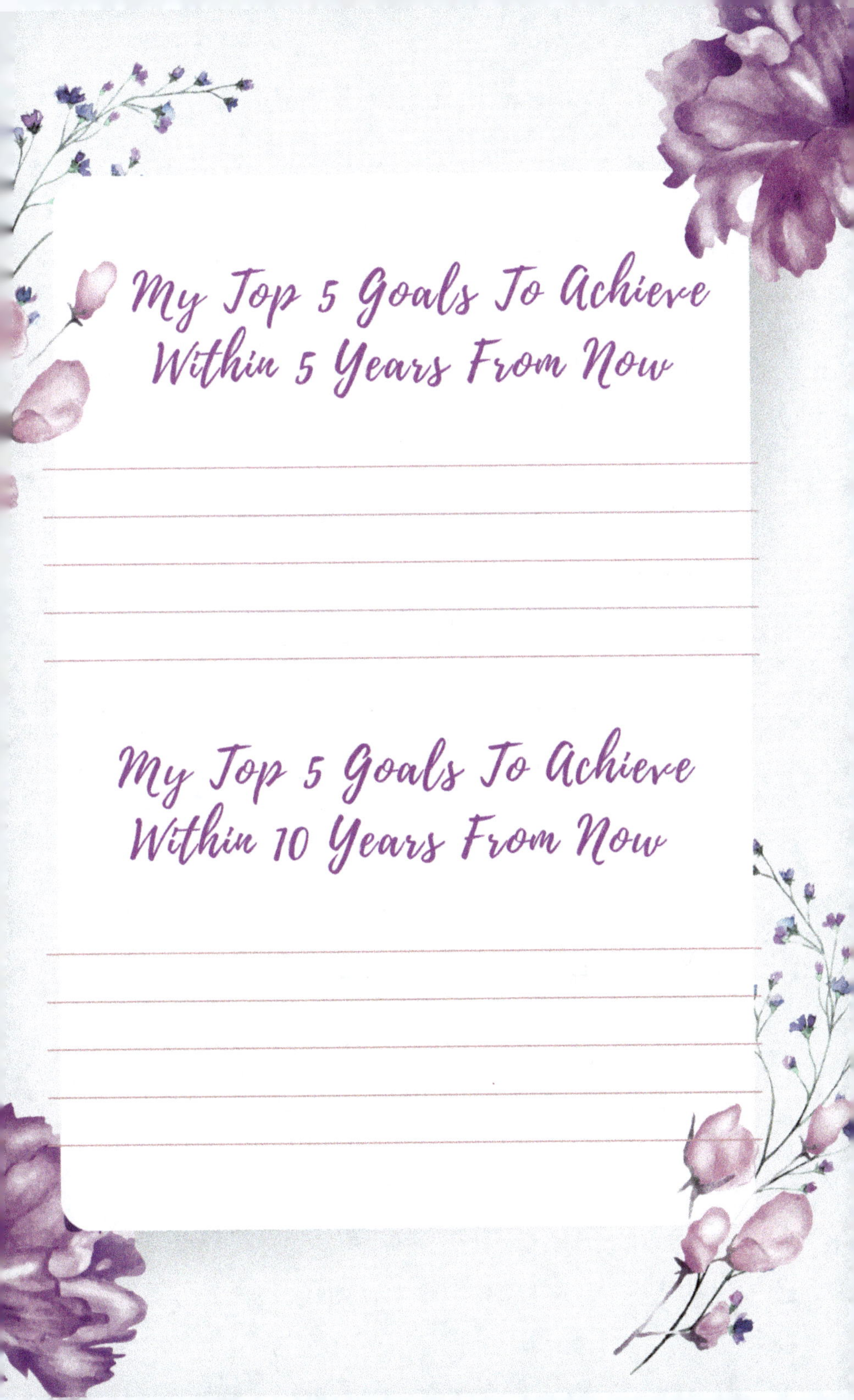

My Top 5 Goals To Achieve Within 5 Years From Now

My Top 5 Goals To Achieve Within 10 Years From Now

My Top Ten Achievements So Far

My Answered Prayers

The Most Important
People in My Life

Please Share Your Feedback About 365 Days Of Bliss Journal

I have always dreamed of creating a unique, vibrant, and inspirational journal for women that can be used throughout the year. This journal is made for all ladies who (like me) would like to jot down their dreams, gratitude, moods, and thoughts each day in a beautiful book that can be carried in a handbag or sit beautifully on the bedside table. I sincerely hope you like this journal which is a true labor of love and dedication of 100s of hours.

People judge a book not just by its cover but also by the reviews! If you have loved this journal, would you please take a moment now and leave your feedback? I promise you it will not cost you any money and will take you less than 60 seconds.

Your review can help this journal reach more ladies like yourself.
All you need to do is, scan the below QR code and leave your feedback.
You could also go to the web page on which you bought this book, and there will be an option to leave a review.

Kindly Note: *This QR code is for US-based Amazon customers.*
If you are from another area (eg. Canada or UK), after you scan the QR code, simply change the ".com" in the website URL to your respective region's version of Amazon (eg: .ca or .co.uk or .de or .it or .fr or .es or .ae or .co.jp or .com.au and so on).

I thank you sincerely from the bottom of my heart.
Wishing you awesome days ahead!
Florance

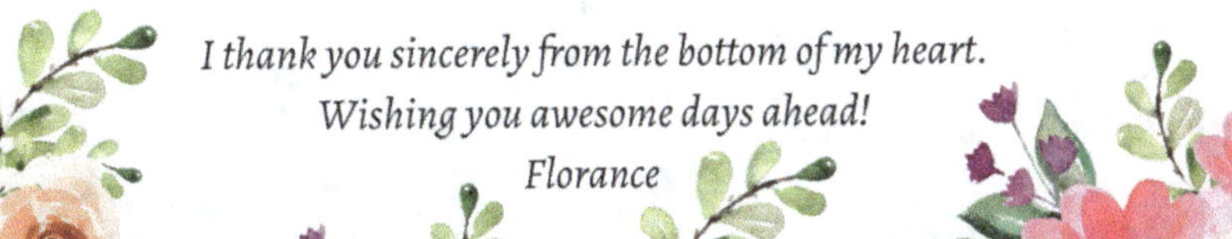

January 1

"If you can dance and be free and be embarrassed, you can rule the world."
- Amy Poehler

Three things I am grateful for today

My goals and dreams

My Affirmation for today

My thoughts for today

How am I feeling today?

\+ –

January 2

"Females are the most beautiful, gorgeous creatures in the whole world. And I think that we are gorgeous no matter what size we are." - Alicia Keys

Three things I am grateful for today

My goals and dreams

My Affirmation for today

My thoughts for today

How am I feeling today?

+ −

January 3

"If you want something said, ask a man. If you want something done, ask a woman."
- Margaret Thatcher

Three things I am grateful for today

My goals and dreams

My Affirmation for today

My thoughts for today

How am I feeling today?

\+ –

January 4

"Gratitude is not only the greatest of virtues but the parent of all others."
- Marcus Tullius Cicero

Three things I am grateful for today

My goals and dreams

My Affirmation for today

My thoughts for today

How am I feeling today?

\+ –

January 5

"You are who you are when nobody's watching."
- Stephen Fry

Three things I am grateful for today

My goals and dreams

My Affirmation for today

My thoughts for today

How am I feeling today?

January 6

"A leader is one who knows the way, goes the way, and shows the way."

- John Maxwell

Three things I am grateful for today

My goals and dreams

My Affirmation for today

My thoughts for today

How am I feeling today?

January 7

"How to stop time: kiss. How to travel in time: read. How to escape time: music. How to feel time: write. How to release time: breathe." - Matt Haig

Three things I am grateful for today

My goals and dreams

My Affirmation for today

My thoughts for today

How am I feeling today?

\+ –

"A single act of kindness throws out roots in all directions, and the roots spring up and make new trees." - Amelia Earhart

Three things I am grateful for today

My goals and dreams

My Affirmation for today

My thoughts for today

How am I feeling today?

\+ −

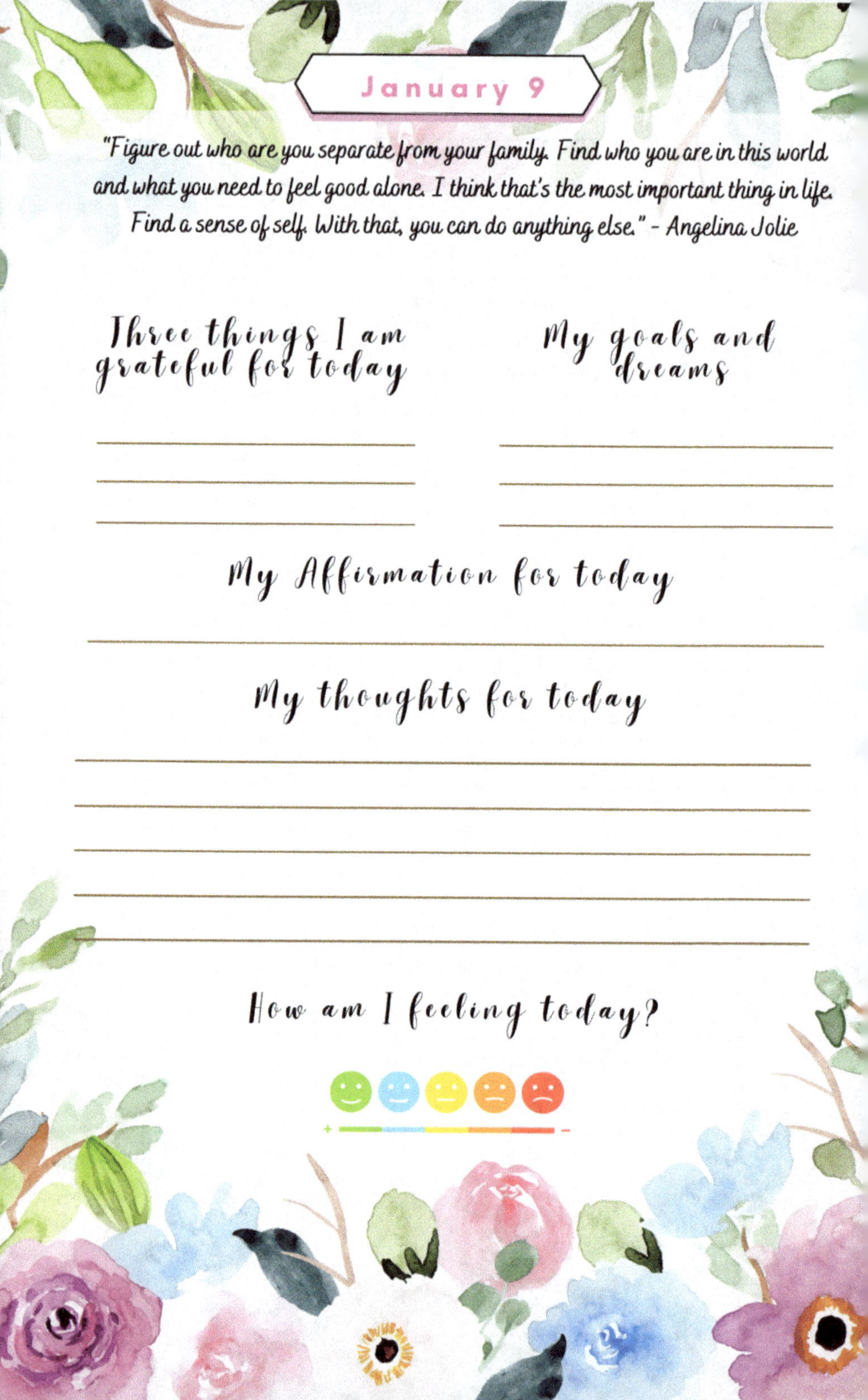

January 9

"Figure out who are you separate from your family. Find who you are in this world and what you need to feel good alone. I think that's the most important thing in life. Find a sense of self. With that, you can do anything else." - Angelina Jolie

Three things I am grateful for today

My goals and dreams

My Affirmation for today

My thoughts for today

How am I feeling today?

+ −

January 10

"It's not about having enough time, it's about making enough time."
- Rachael Bermingham

Three things I am grateful for today

My goals and dreams

My Affirmation for today

My thoughts for today

How am I feeling today?

"Do not follow where the path may lead. Go instead where there is no path and leave a trail." - Muriel Strode

Three things I am grateful for today

My goals and dreams

My Affirmation for today

My thoughts for today

How am I feeling today?

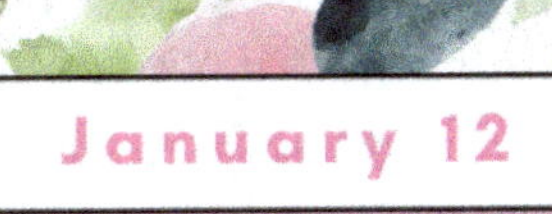

January 12

"I am a woman phenomenally. Phenomenal woman, that's me."
- Maya Angelou

Three things I am grateful for today

My goals and dreams

My Affirmation for today

My thoughts for today

How am I feeling today?

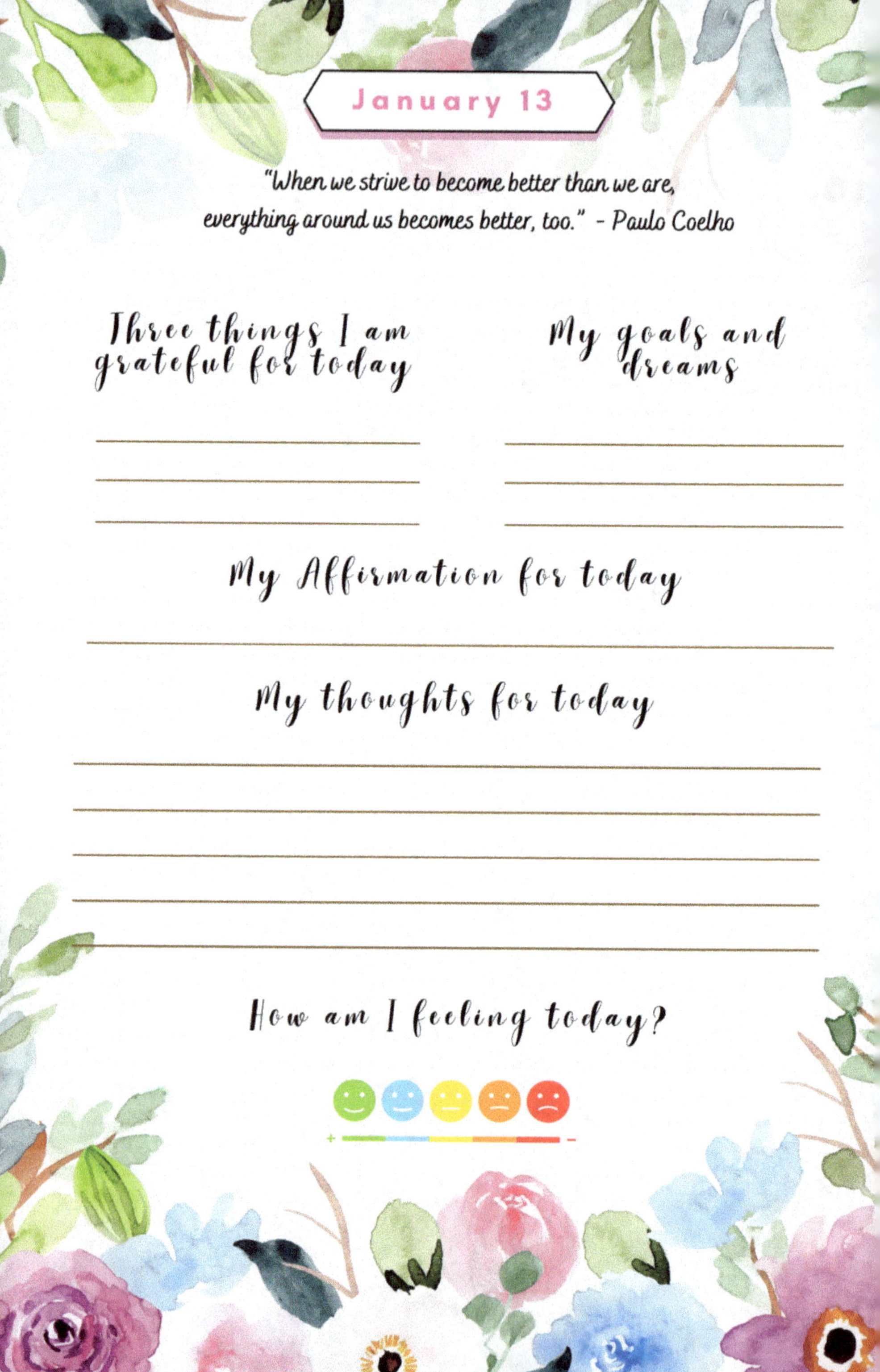

January 13

"When we strive to become better than we are, everything around us becomes better, too." - Paulo Coelho

Three things I am grateful for today

My goals and dreams

My Affirmation for today

My thoughts for today

How am I feeling today?

+ –

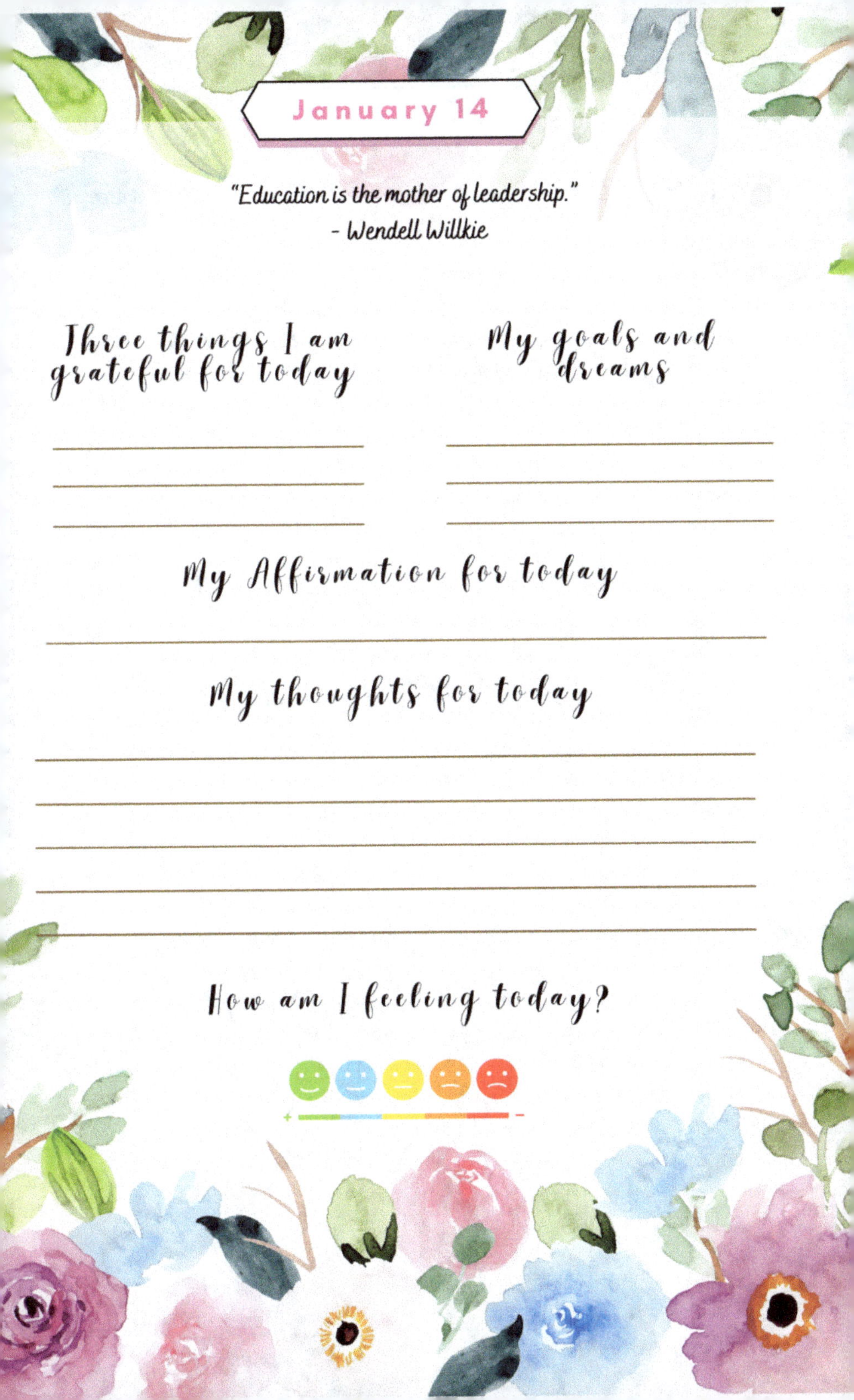

January 14

"Education is the mother of leadership."
- Wendell Willkie

Three things I am grateful for today

My goals and dreams

My Affirmation for today

My thoughts for today

How am I feeling today?

January 15

"It is better to be hated for what you are than to be loved for what you are not."
- André Gide

Three things I am grateful for today

My goals and dreams

My Affirmation for today

My thoughts for today

How am I feeling today?

\+ –

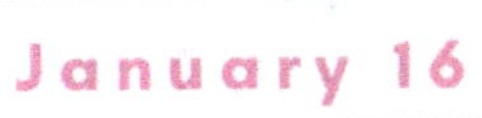

"Don't feel stupid if you don't like what everyone else pretends to love."

- Emma Watson

Three things I am grateful for today

My goals and dreams

My Affirmation for today

My thoughts for today

How am I feeling today?

"You are never too small to make a difference."
- Greta Thunberg

Three things I am grateful for today

My goals and dreams

My Affirmation for today

My thoughts for today

How am I feeling today?

+ –

January 18

"Nothing can be done without hope and confidence."
- Helen Keller

Three things I am grateful for today

My goals and dreams

My Affirmation for today

My thoughts for today

How am I feeling today?

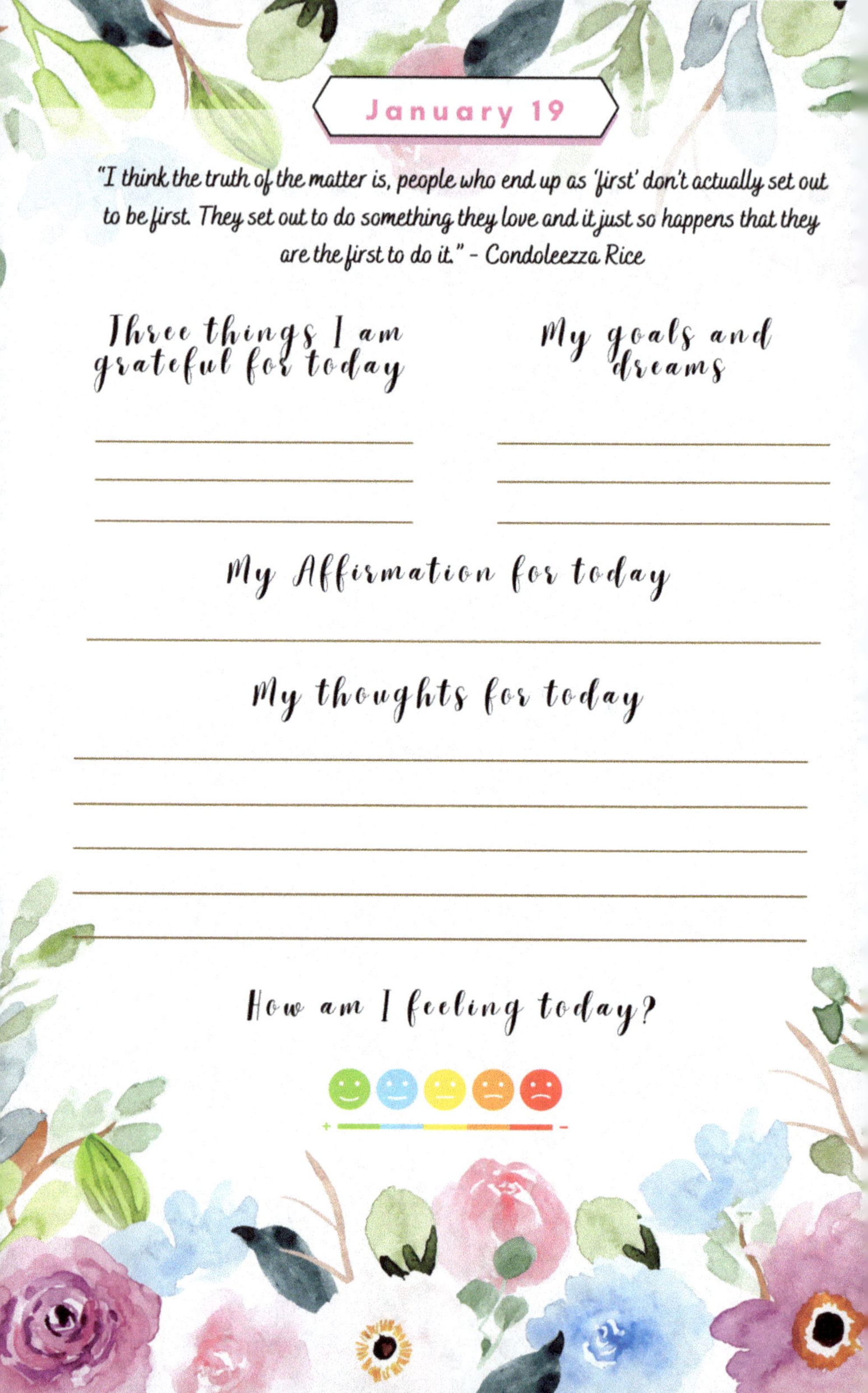

January 19

"I think the truth of the matter is, people who end up as 'first' don't actually set out to be first. They set out to do something they love and it just so happens that they are the first to do it." - Condoleezza Rice

Three things I am grateful for today

My goals and dreams

My Affirmation for today

My thoughts for today

How am I feeling today?

+ –

January 20

"Courage starts with showing up and letting ourselves be seen."
- Brené Brown

Three things I am grateful for today

My goals and dreams

My Affirmation for today

My thoughts for today

How am I feeling today?

+ –

January 21

"It takes nothing to join the crowd. It takes everything to stand alone."
- Hans F. Hansen

Three things I am grateful for today

My goals and dreams

My Affirmation for today

My thoughts for today

How am I feeling today?

+ –

January 22

"Innovation distinguishes between a leader and a follower."
- Steve Jobs

Three things I am grateful for today

My goals and dreams

My Affirmation for today

My thoughts for today

How am I feeling today?

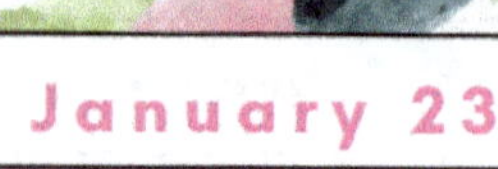

January 23

"Above all, be the heroine of your life, not the victim."
- Nora Ephron

Three things I am grateful for today

My goals and dreams

My Affirmation for today

My thoughts for today

How am I feeling today?

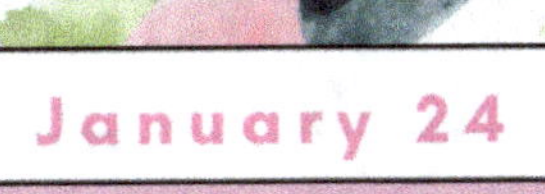

"The greatest gift you could give someone is your time. Because when you give your time, you are giving a portion of your life you can't get back." - Unknown

Three things I am grateful for today

My goals and dreams

My Affirmation for today

My thoughts for today

How am I feeling today?

\+ –

"When one door of happiness closes, another opens; but often we look so long at the closed door that we do not see the one which has been opened for us."

- Helen Keller

Three things I am grateful for today

My goals and dreams

My Affirmation for today

My thoughts for today

How am I feeling today?

\+ –

January 26

"You can't let your failures define you. You have to let your failures teach you."
- Barack Obama

Three things I am grateful for today

My goals and dreams

My Affirmation for today

My thoughts for today

How am I feeling today?

+ –

January 27

"Life is like riding a bicycle. To keep your balance, you must keep moving."
- Albert Einstein

Three things I am grateful for today

My goals and dreams

My Affirmation for today

My thoughts for today

How am I feeling today?

January 28

"Self-confidence is the memory of success."
- David Storey

Three things I am grateful for today

My goals and dreams

My Affirmation for today

My thoughts for today

How am I feeling today?

"I believe in being strong when everything seems to be going wrong. I believe that happy girls are the prettiest girls. I believe that tomorrow is another day, and I believe in miracles." - Audrey Hepburn

Three things I am grateful for today

___

___

___

My goals and dreams

___

___

___

My Affirmation for today

___

My thoughts for today

___

___

___

___

___

How am I feeling today?

January 30

"To handle yourself, use your head; to handle others, use your heart."
- Eleanor Roosevelt

Three things I am grateful for today

My goals and dreams

My Affirmation for today

My thoughts for today

How am I feeling today?

\+ –

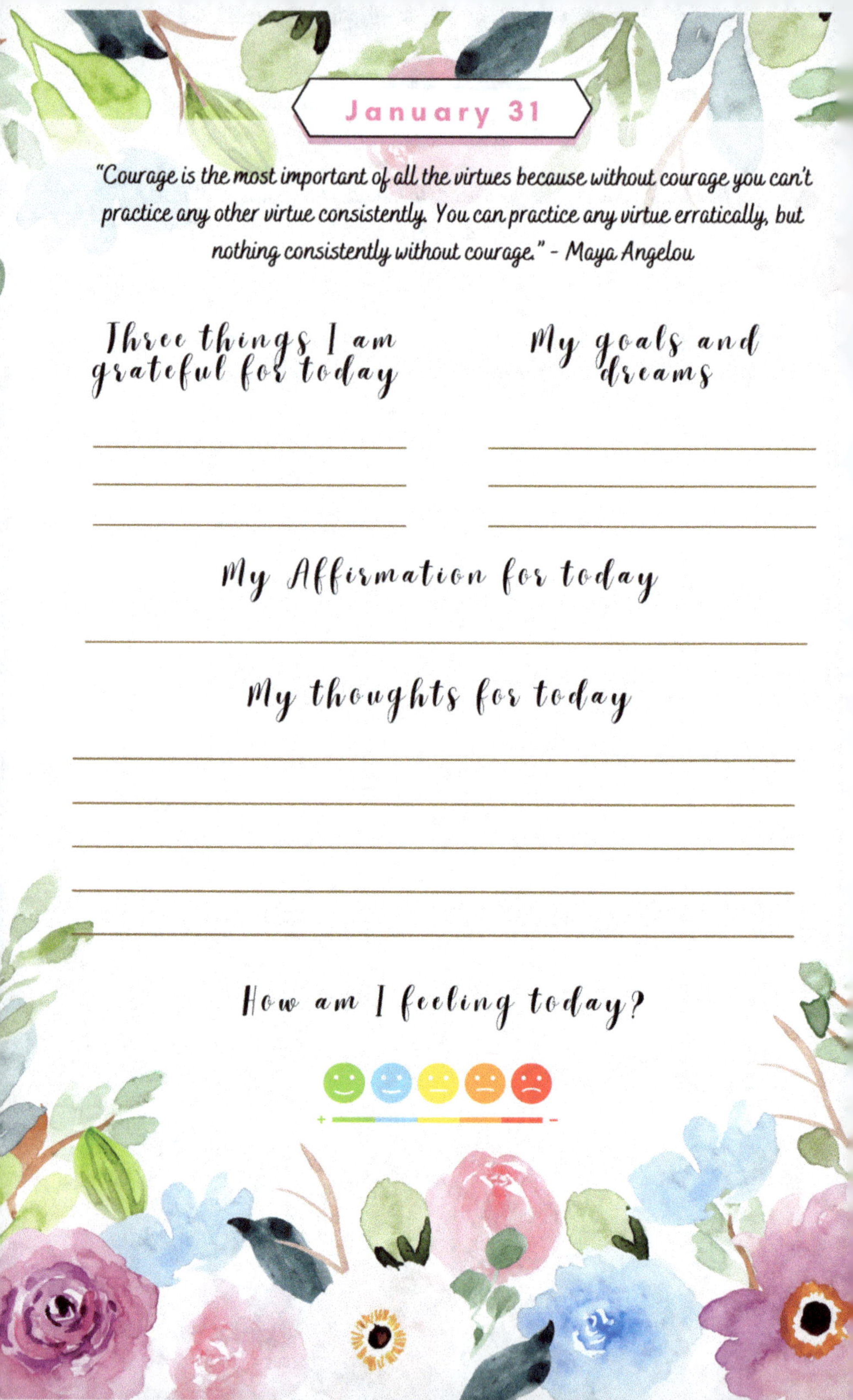

January 31

"Courage is the most important of all the virtues because without courage you can't practice any other virtue consistently. You can practice any virtue erratically, but nothing consistently without courage." - Maya Angelou

Three things I am grateful for today

My goals and dreams

My Affirmation for today

My thoughts for today

How am I feeling today?

February 1

"There is a calmness to a life lived in gratitude, a quiet joy."
- Ralph H. Blum

Three things I am grateful for

My goals and dreams

My Affirmation for today

My thoughts for today

How am I feeling today?

February 2

"The best time to plant a tree was 20 years ago.
The second best time is now." - Chinese Proverb

Three things I am grateful for

___

___

___

My goals and dreams

___

___

___

My Affirmation for today

___

My thoughts for today

___

___

___

___

___

How am I feeling today?

\+ −

February 3

"Failure isn't the end of the road. It's a big red flag saying to you 'Wrong way. Turn around.'" - Oprah Winfrey

Three things I am grateful for

My goals and dreams

My Affirmation for today

My thoughts for today

How am I feeling today?

February 4

"The confidence which we have in ourselves gives birth to much of that which we have in others." - François de La Rochefoucauld

Three things I am grateful for

My goals and dreams

My Affirmation for today

My thoughts for today

How am I feeling today?

February 5

"To love yourself is a never-ending journey." - Oprah Winfrey

Three things I am grateful for

My goals and dreams

My Affirmation for today

My thoughts for today

How am I feeling today?

+ −

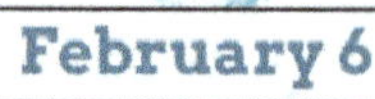

February 6

"To kindness and love, the things we need most." - The Grinch

Three things I am grateful for

My goals and dreams

My Affirmation for today

My thoughts for today

How am I feeling today?

February 7

"If people are doubting how far you can go, go so far that you can't hear them anymore." - Michele Ruiz

Three things I am grateful for

____

____

____

My goals and dreams

____

____

____

My Affirmation for today

____

My thoughts for today

____

____

____

____

____

How am I feeling today?

February 8

"We are all faced with a series of great opportunities brilliantly disguised as impossible situations." - Chuck Swindoll

Three things I am grateful for

My goals and dreams

My Affirmation for today

My thoughts for today

How am I feeling today?

February 9

"Do one thing every day that scares you." - Eleanor Roosevelt

Three things I am grateful for

___

___

___

My goals and dreams

___

___

___

My Affirmation for today

___

My thoughts for today

___

___

___

___

___

How am I feeling today?

+ −

February 10

"There's something special about a woman who dominates in a man's world. It takes a certain grace, strength, intelligence, fearlessness, and the nerve to never take no for an answer." - Rihanna

Three things I am grateful for

___

___

___

My goals and dreams

___

___

___

My Affirmation for today

___

My thoughts for today

___

___

___

___

___

How am I feeling today?

February 11

"Trust yourself—you know more than you think you do."
- Benjamin Spock

Three things I am grateful for

My goals and dreams

My Affirmation for today

My thoughts for today

How am I feeling today?

February 12

"Gratitude will shift you to a higher frequency, and you will attract much better things." - Rhonda Byrne

Three things I am grateful for

My goals and dreams

My Affirmation for today

My thoughts for today

How am I feeling today?

February 13

"The hard days are what make you stronger." - Aly Raisman

Three things I am grateful for

____

____

____

My goals and dreams

____

____

____

My Affirmation for today

____

My thoughts for today

____

____

____

____

____

How am I feeling today?

February 14

"Gratitude for the present moment and the fullness of life now is the true prosperity." - Eckhart Tolle

Three things I am grateful for

___

___

___

My goals and dreams

___

___

___

My Affirmation for today

___

My thoughts for today

___

___

___

___

___

How am I feeling today?

February 15

"If your actions inspire others to dream more, learn more, do more and become more, you are a leader." - John Quincy Adams

Three things I am grateful for

____

____

____

My goals and dreams

____

____

____

My Affirmation for today

____

My thoughts for today

____

____

____

____

____

How am I feeling today?

February 16

"All our dreams can come true, if we have the courage to pursue them." - Walt Disney

Three things I am grateful for

My goals and dreams

My Affirmation for today

My thoughts for today

How am I feeling today?

February 17

"Happiness is something that multiplies when it is divided." - Paulo Coelho

Three things I am grateful for

____

____

____

My goals and dreams

____

____

____

My Affirmation for today

____

My thoughts for today

____

____

____

____

____

How am I feeling today?

\+ –

"When the going gets tough, the tough get going." - Joe Kennedy

Three things I am grateful for

My goals and dreams

My Affirmation for today

My thoughts for today

February 19

"If you believe it'll work out, you'll see opportunities. If you don't believe it'll work out, you'll see obstacles." - Wayne Dyer

Three things I am grateful for

My goals and dreams

My Affirmation for today

My thoughts for today

How am I feeling today?

February 20

"Make improvements, not excuses. Seek respect, not attention."
- Roy T. Bennett

Three things I am grateful for

___

___

___

My goals and dreams

___

___

___

My Affirmation for today

___

My thoughts for today

___

___

___

___

___

How am I feeling today?

February 21

"Someone is sitting in the shade today because someone planted a tree a long time ago." - Warren Buffett

Three things I am grateful for

____

____

____

My goals and dreams

____

____

____

My Affirmation for today

____

My thoughts for today

____

____

____

____

____

How am I feeling today?

February 22

"You've gotta dance like there's nobody watching, love like you'll never be hurt, sing like there's nobody listening, and live like it's heaven on earth - William W. Purkey

Three things I am grateful for

____

____

____

My goals and dreams

____

____

____

My Affirmation for today

____

My thoughts for today

____

____

____

____

____

How am I feeling today?

February 23

"He is a wise man who does not grieve for the things which he has not, but rejoices for those which he has" - Epictetus

Three things I am grateful for

My goals and dreams

My Affirmation for today

My thoughts for today

How am I feeling today?

February 24

"Keep your eyes on the stars, and your feet on the ground."
- Theodore Roosevelt

Three things I am grateful for

____

____

____

My goals and dreams

____

____

____

My Affirmation for today

____

My thoughts for today

____

____

____

____

____

How am I feeling today?

February 25

"You can waste your lives drawing lines. Or you can live your life crossing them" - Shonda Rhimes

Three things I am grateful for

My goals and dreams

My Affirmation for today

My thoughts for today

How am I feeling today?

February 26

"Luck is believing you're lucky." - Tennessee Williams

Three things I am grateful for

My goals and dreams

My Affirmation for today

My thoughts for today

How am I feeling today?

February 27

"The secret of getting ahead is getting started."
- Mark Twain

three things I am grateful for

My goals and dreams

My Affirmation for today

My thoughts for today

How am I feeling today?

February 28

"Fairy tales are more than true: not because they tell us that dragons exist, but because they tell us that dragons can be beaten." - Neil Gaiman

Three things I am grateful for

___
___
___

My goals and dreams

___
___
___

My Affirmation for today

___

My thoughts for today

___
___
___
___
___

How am I feeling today?

February 29

"How wonderful it is that nobody needs to wait a single moment before starting to improve the world." - Anne Frank

Three things I am grateful for

My goals and dreams

My Affirmation for today

My thoughts for today

How am I feeling today?

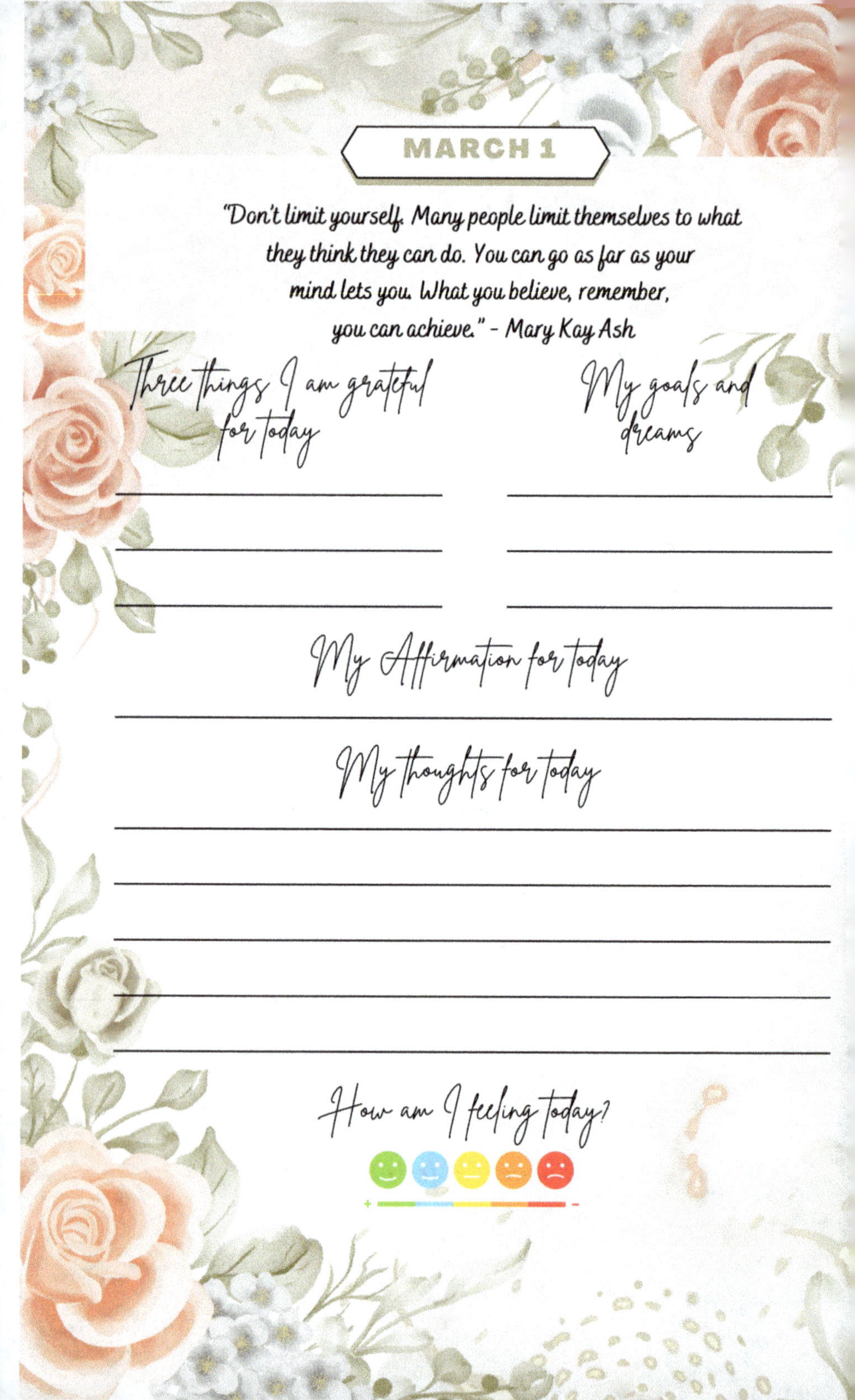

MARCH 1

"Don't limit yourself. Many people limit themselves to what they think they can do. You can go as far as your mind lets you. What you believe, remember, you can achieve." - Mary Kay Ash

Three things I am grateful for today

My goals and dreams

My Affirmation for today

My thoughts for today

How am I feeling today?

MARCH 2

"It's hard to beat a person who never gives up."
- Babe Ruth

Three things I am grateful for today

My goals and dreams

My Affirmation for today

My thoughts for today

How am I feeling today?

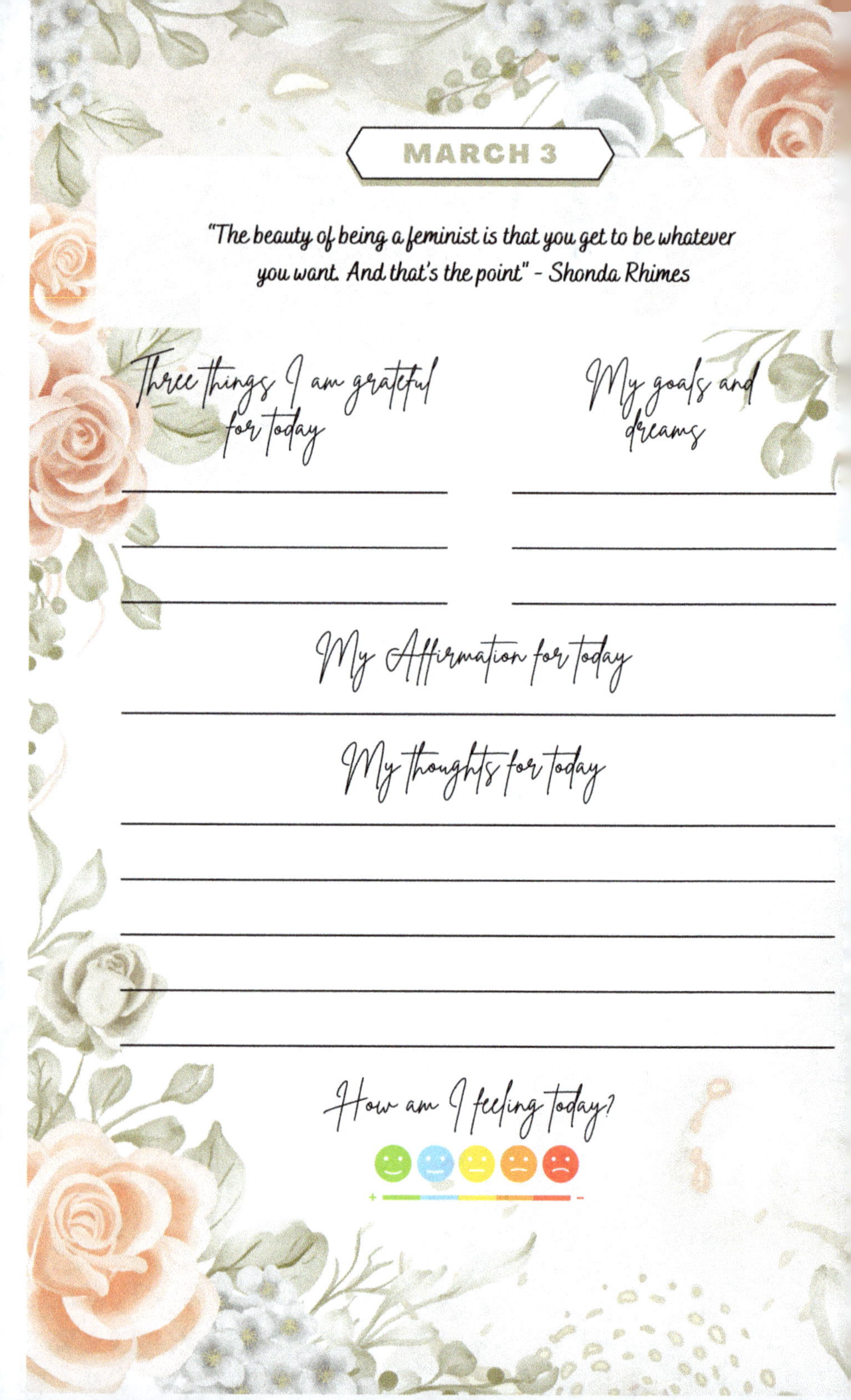

MARCH 3

"The beauty of being a feminist is that you get to be whatever you want. And that's the point" - Shonda Rhimes

Three things I am grateful for today

My goals and dreams

My Affirmation for today

My thoughts for today

How am I feeling today?

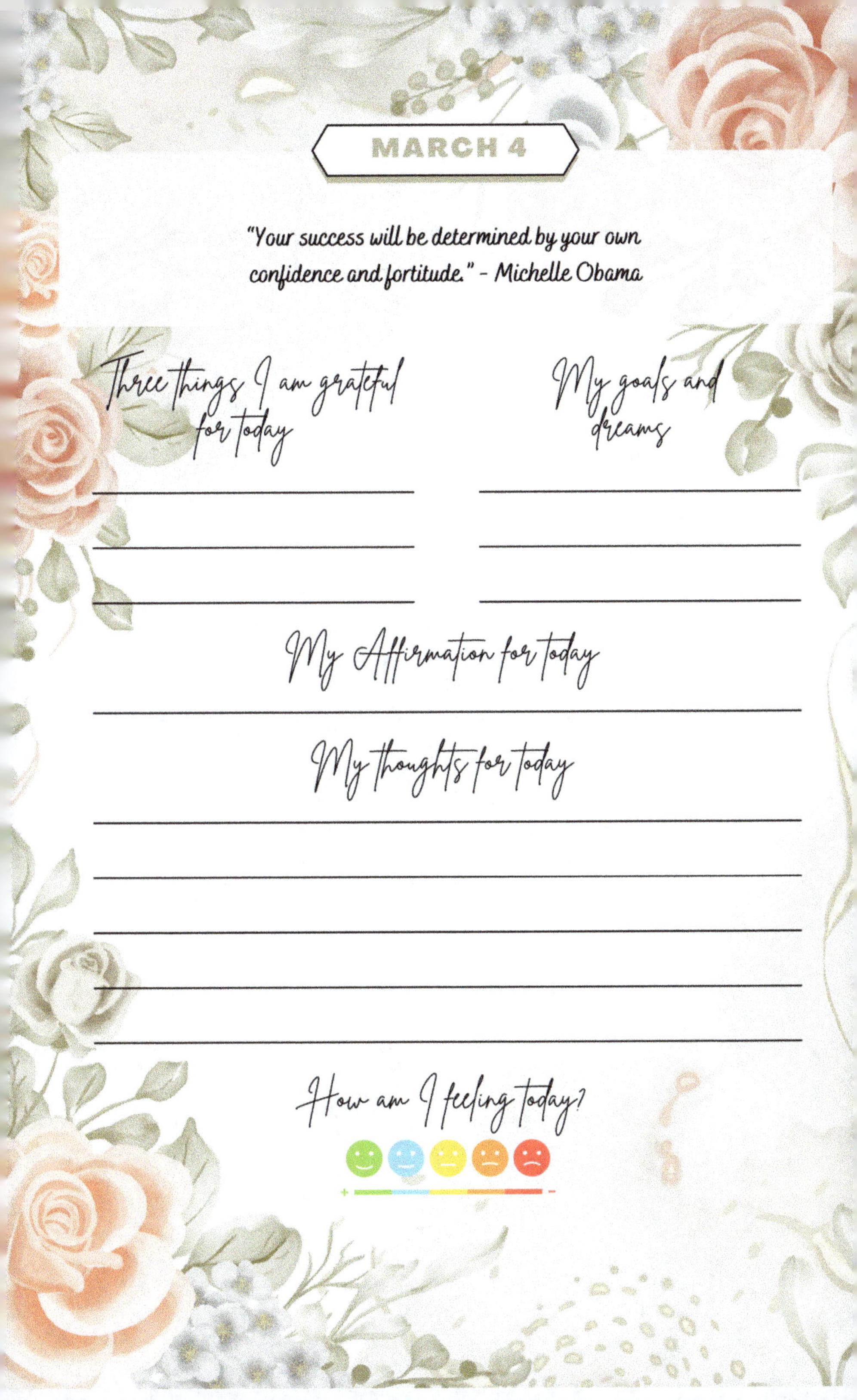

MARCH 4

"Your success will be determined by your own confidence and fortitude." - Michelle Obama

Three things I am grateful for today

My goals and dreams

My Affirmation for today

My thoughts for today

How am I feeling today?

+ –

MARCH 5

"Some people want it to happen, some wish it would happen, others make it happen" - Michael Jordan

Three things I am grateful for today

My goals and dreams

My Affirmation for today

My thoughts for today

How am I feeling today?

+ –

MARCH 6

"I'm a greater believer in luck, and I find the harder I work the more I have of it" - Thomas Jefferson

Three things I am grateful for today

My goals and dreams

My Affirmation for today

My thoughts for today

How am I feeling today?

\+ −

MARCH 7

"Great things are done by a series of small things brought together" - Vincent Van Gogh

Three things I am grateful for today

My goals and dreams

My Affirmation for today

My thoughts for today

How am I feeling today?

MARCH 8

"Women are like teabags. We don't know our true strength until we are in hot water" - Eleanor Roosevelt

Three things I am grateful for today

My goals and dreams

My Affirmation for today

My thoughts for today

How am I feeling today?

MARCH 9

"You've got to get up every morning with determination if you're going to go to bed with satisfaction." - George Lorimer

Three things I am grateful for today

My goals and dreams

My Affirmation for today

My thoughts for today

How am I feeling today?

+ –

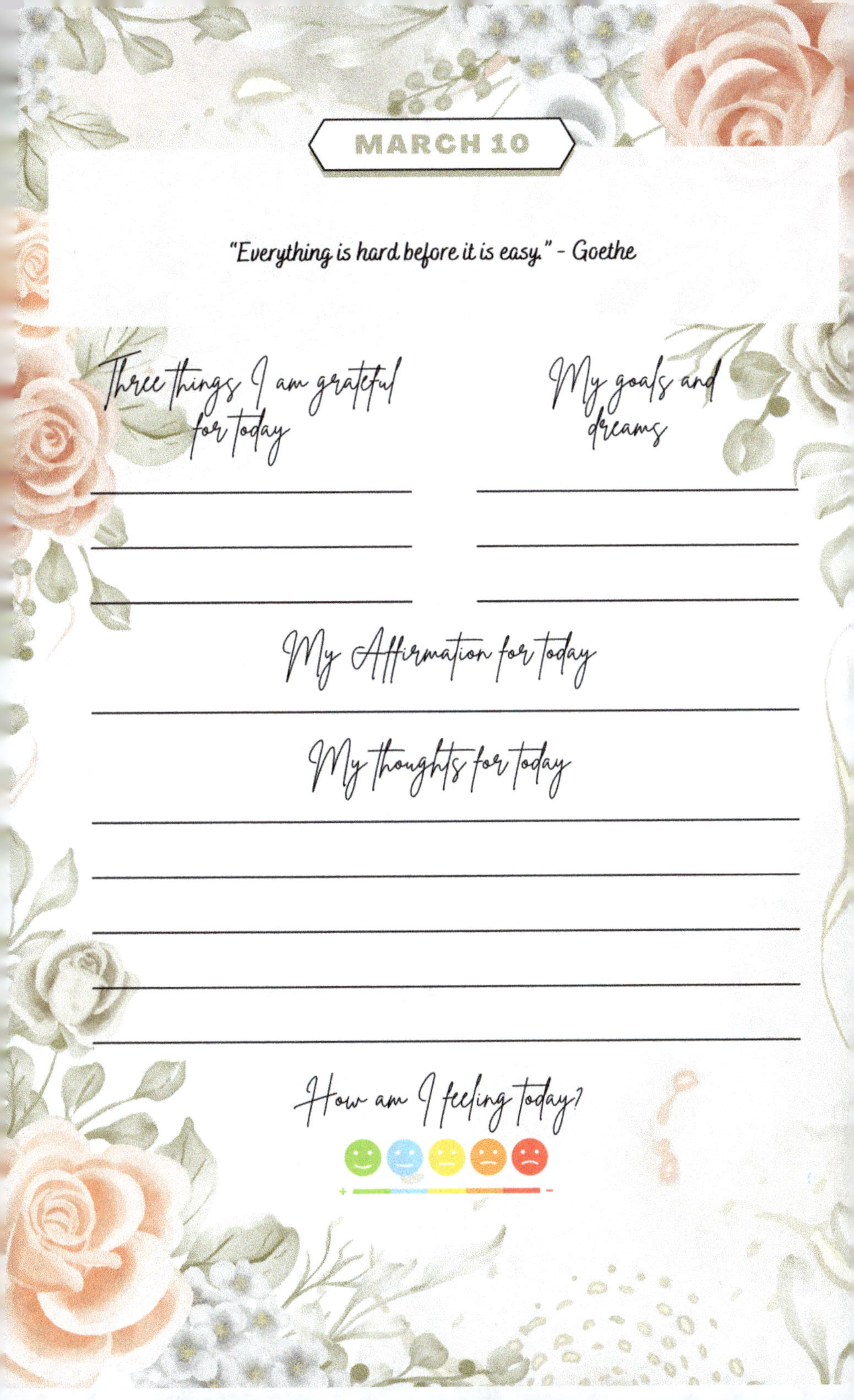

MARCH 10

"Everything is hard before it is easy." - Goethe

Three things I am grateful for today

My goals and dreams

My Affirmation for today

My thoughts for today

How am I feeling today?

+ –

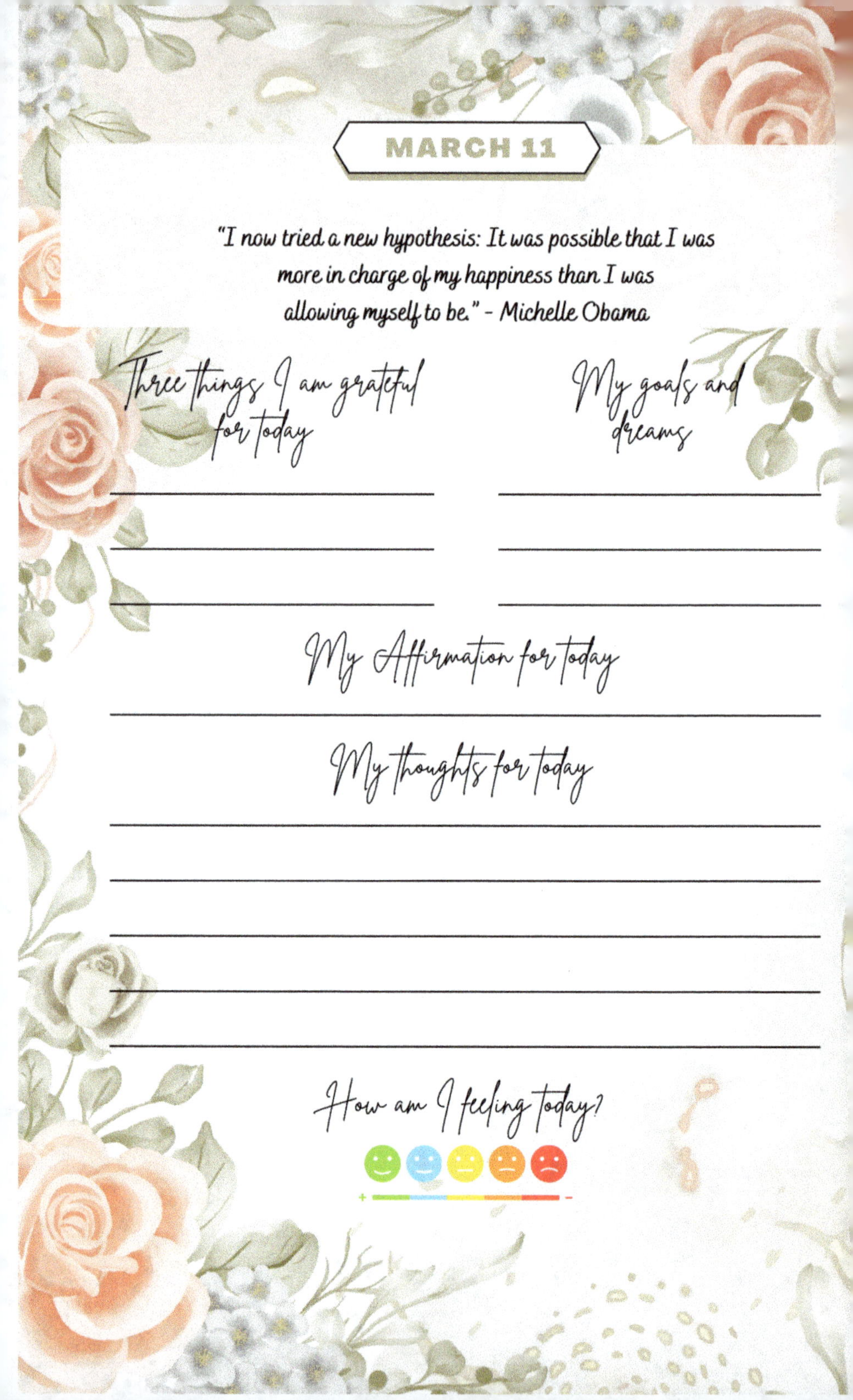

MARCH 11

"I now tried a new hypothesis: It was possible that I was more in charge of my happiness than I was allowing myself to be." - Michelle Obama

Three things I am grateful for today

My goals and dreams

My Affirmation for today

My thoughts for today

How am I feeling today?

+ –

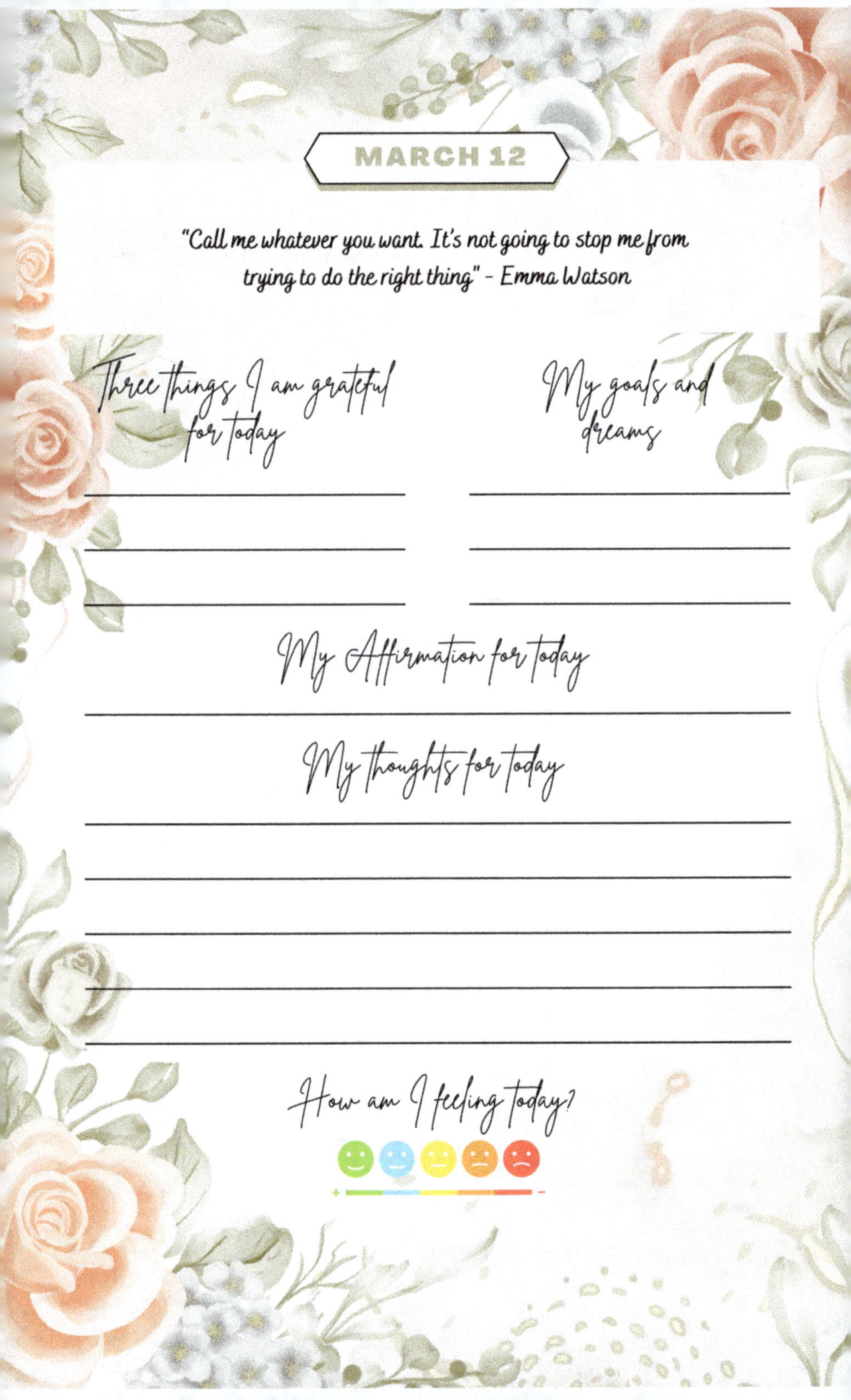

MARCH 12

"Call me whatever you want. It's not going to stop me from trying to do the right thing" - Emma Watson

Three things I am grateful for today

My goals and dreams

My Affirmation for today

My thoughts for today

How am I feeling today?

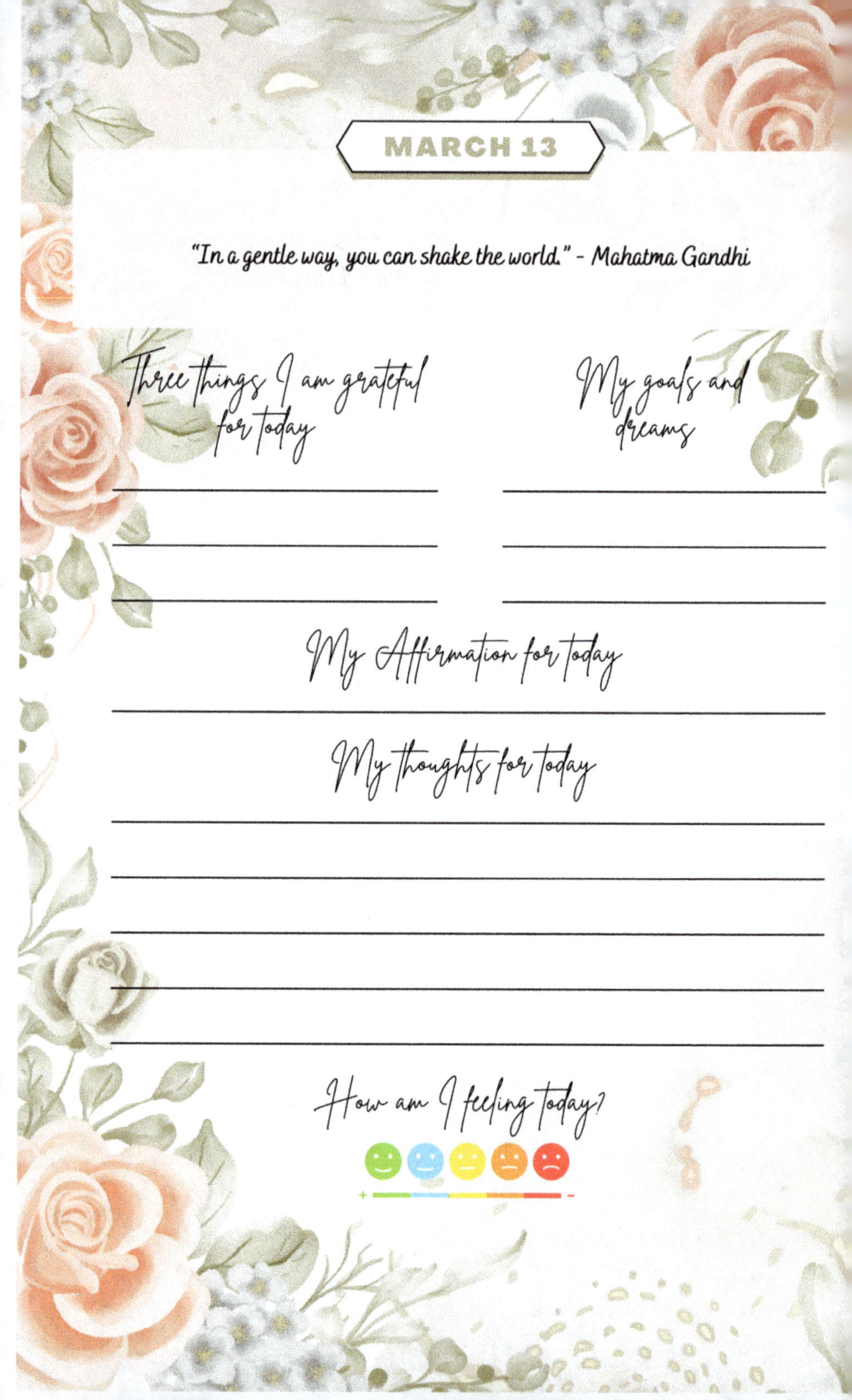

MARCH 13

"In a gentle way, you can shake the world." - Mahatma Gandhi

Three things I am grateful for today

My goals and dreams

My Affirmation for today

My thoughts for today

How am I feeling today?

+ -

MARCH 14

"If opportunity doesn't knock, build a door." - Kurt Cobain

Three things I am grateful for today

My goals and dreams

My Affirmation for today

My thoughts for today

How am I feeling today?

MARCH 15

"Kindness is the language which the deaf can hear and the blind can see." - Mark Twain

Three things I am grateful for today

My goals and dreams

My Affirmation for today

My thoughts for today

How am I feeling today?

+ –

MARCH 16

"Don't be pushed around by the fears in your mind. Be led by the dreams in your heart." - Roy T. Bennett

Three things I am grateful for today

My goals and dreams

My Affirmation for today

My thoughts for today

How am I feeling today?

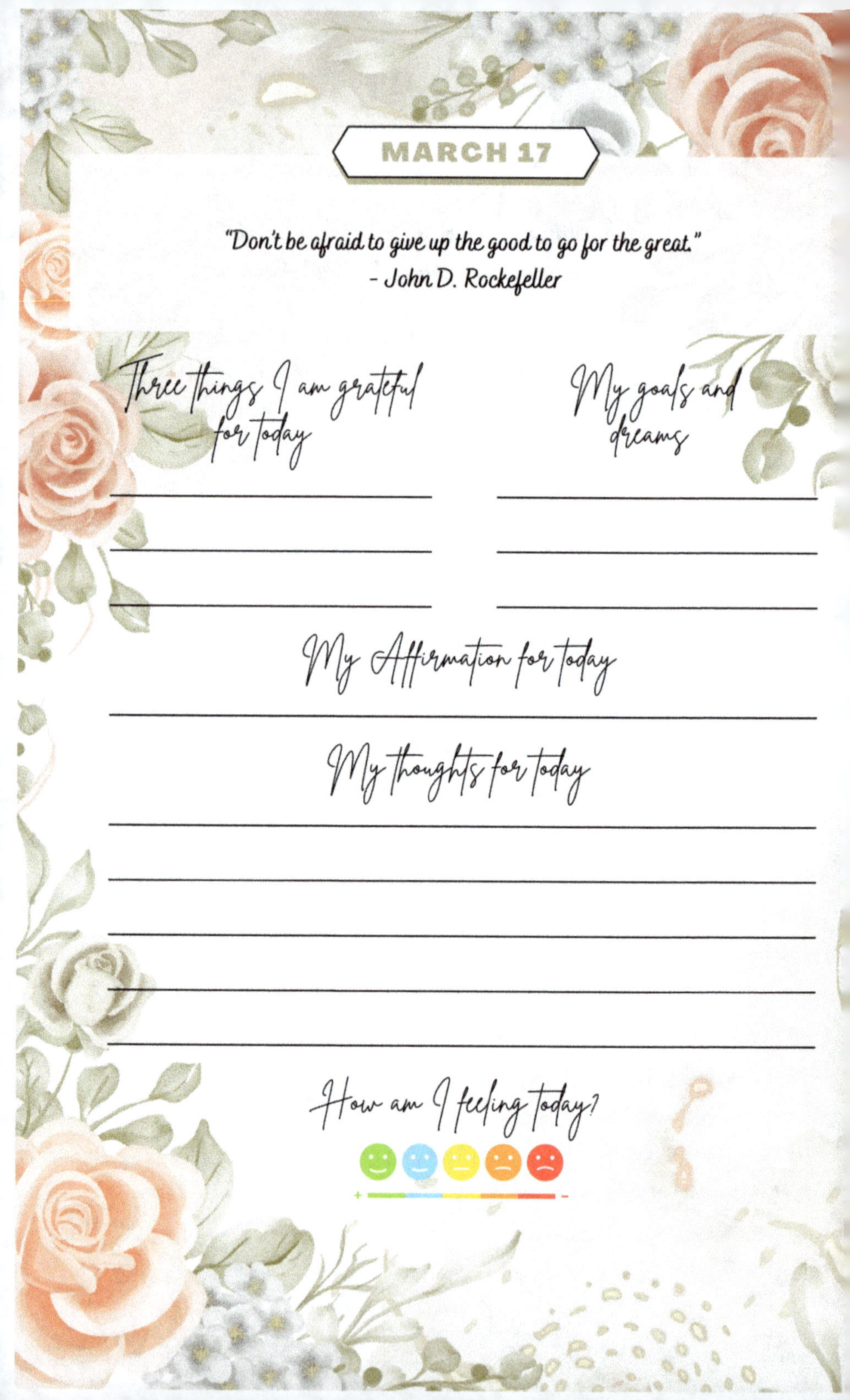

MARCH 17

"Don't be afraid to give up the good to go for the great."
- John D. Rockefeller

Three things I am grateful for today

My goals and dreams

My Affirmation for today

My thoughts for today

How am I feeling today?

+ –

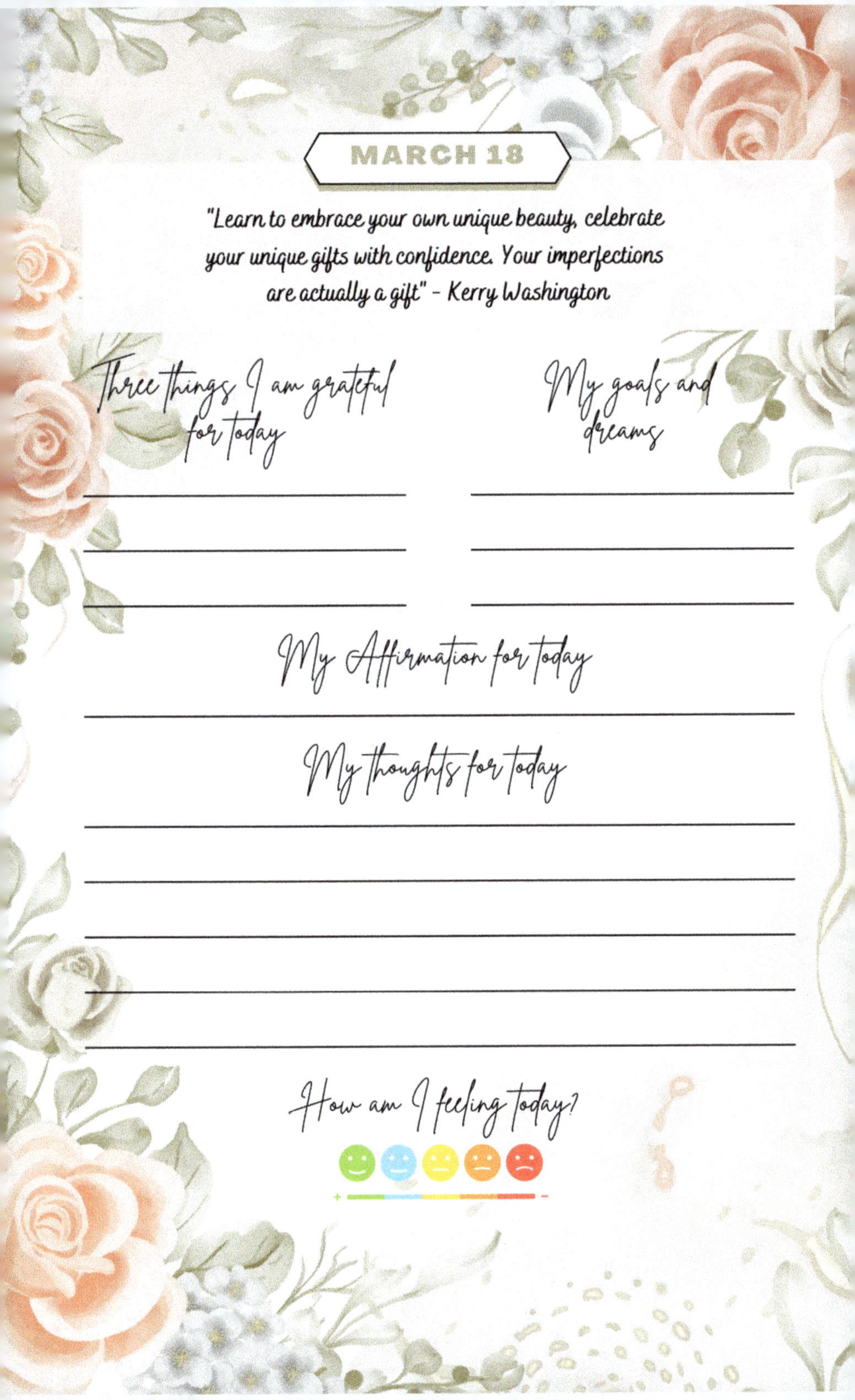

MARCH 18

"Learn to embrace your own unique beauty, celebrate your unique gifts with confidence. Your imperfections are actually a gift" - Kerry Washington

Three things I am grateful for today

My goals and dreams

My Affirmation for today

My thoughts for today

How am I feeling today?

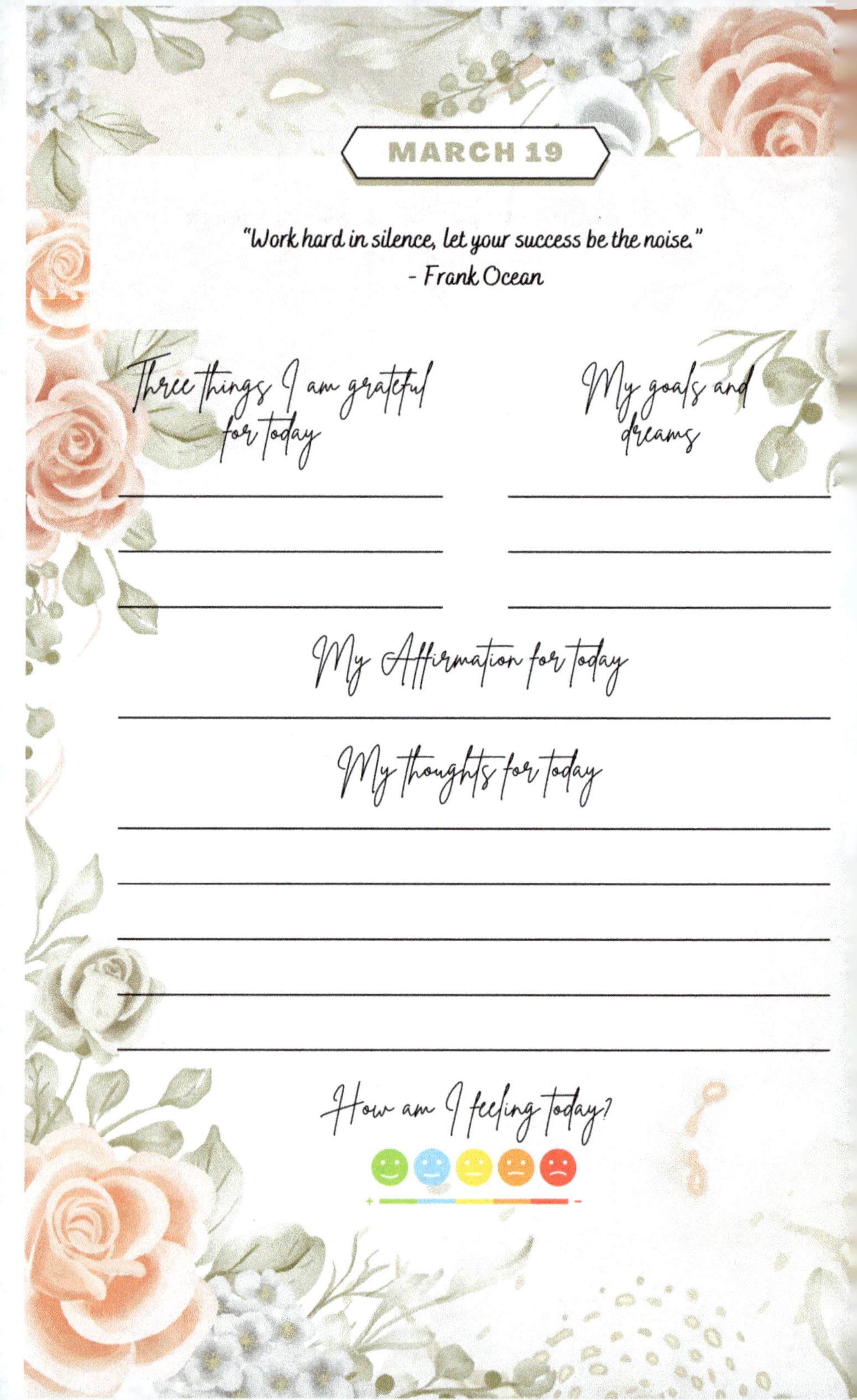

MARCH 19

"Work hard in silence, let your success be the noise."
- Frank Ocean

Three things I am grateful for today

My goals and dreams

My Affirmation for today

My thoughts for today

How am I feeling today?

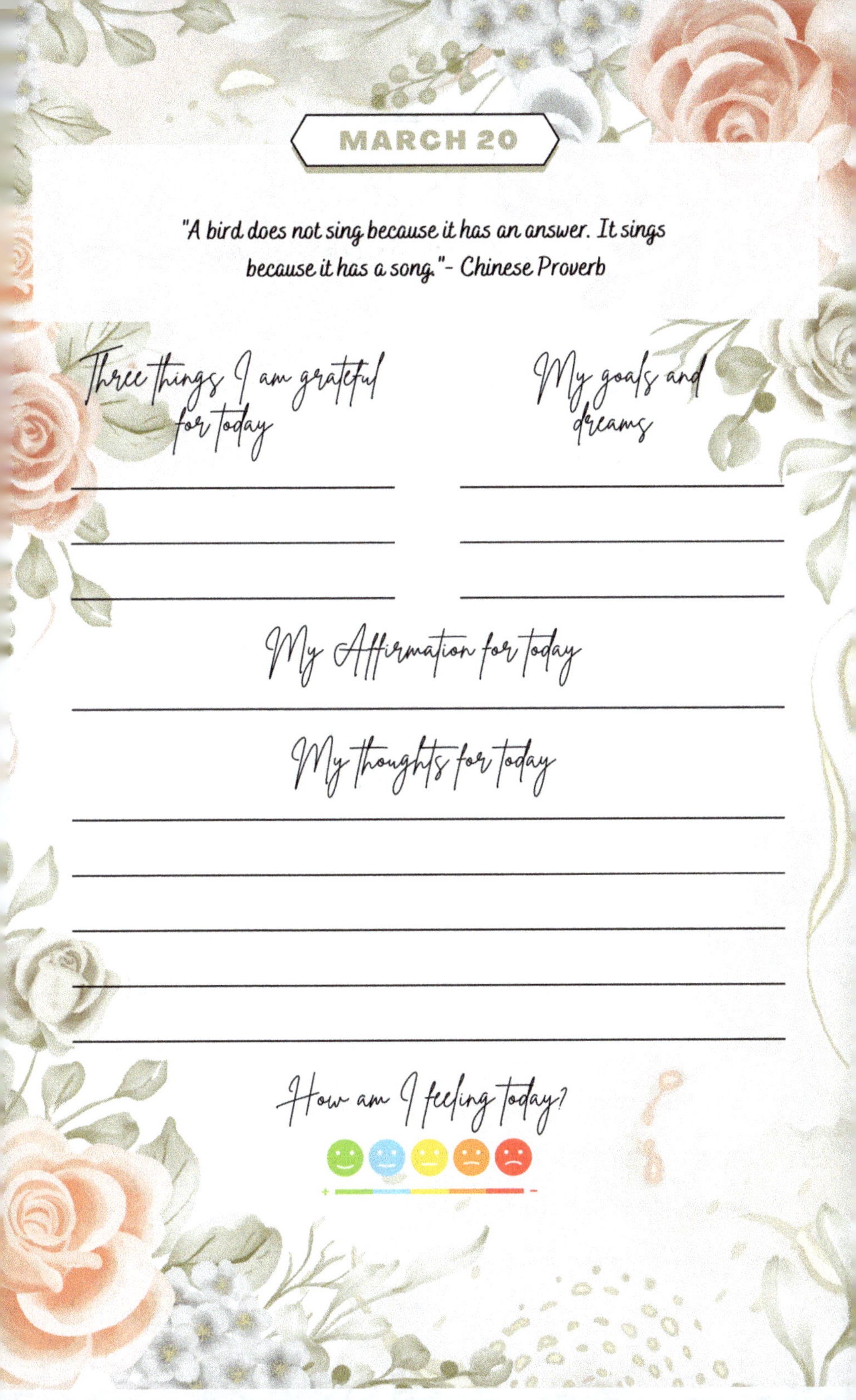

MARCH 20

"A bird does not sing because it has an answer. It sings because it has a song." - Chinese Proverb

Three things I am grateful for today

My goals and dreams

My Affirmation for today

My thoughts for today

How am I feeling today?

MARCH 21

"Am I good enough? Yes, I am." - Michelle Obama

Three things I am grateful for today

My goals and dreams

My Affirmation for today

My thoughts for today

How am I feeling today?

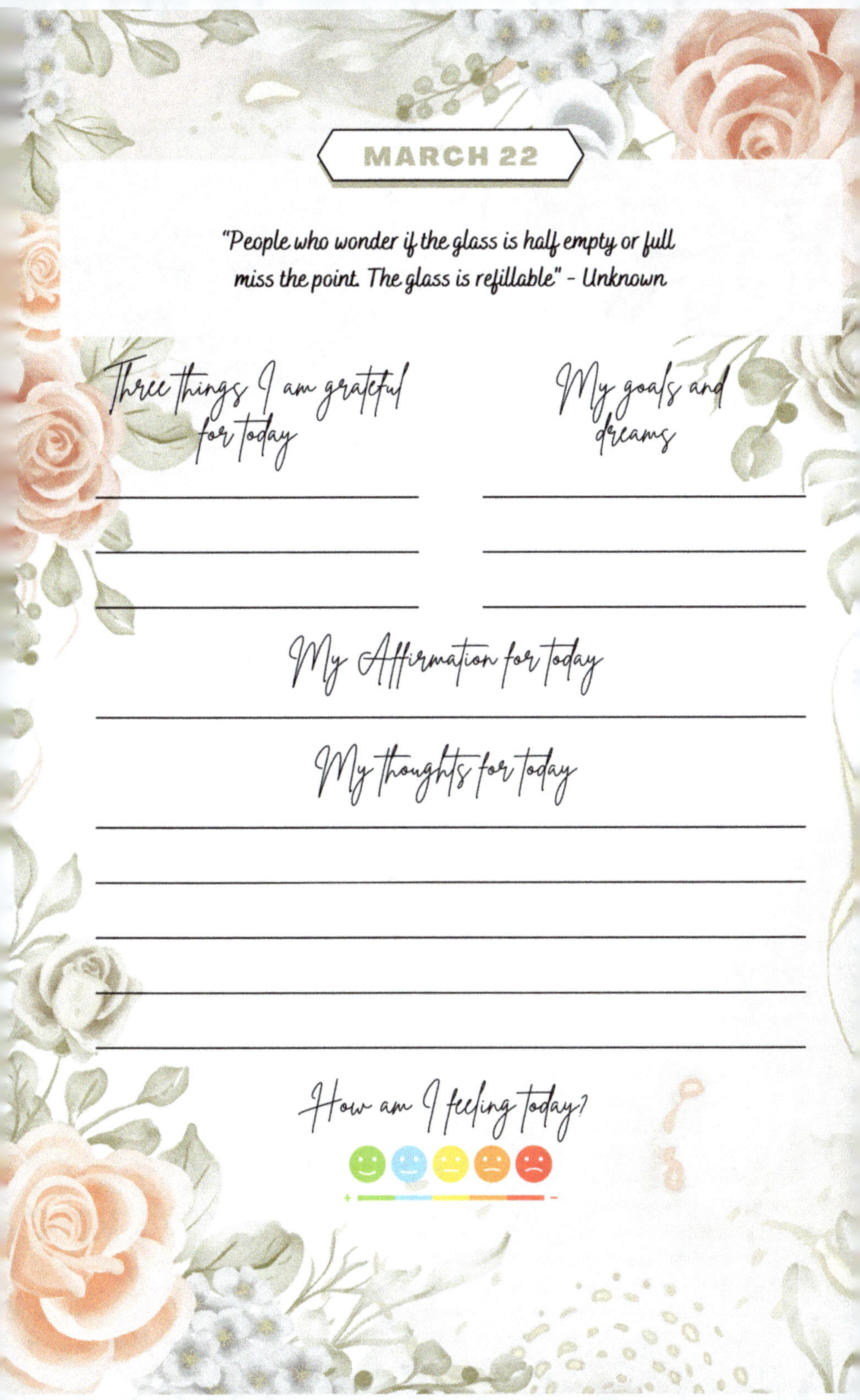

MARCH 22

"People who wonder if the glass is half empty or full miss the point. The glass is refillable" - Unknown

Three things I am grateful for today

My goals and dreams

My Affirmation for today

My thoughts for today

How am I feeling today?

+ –

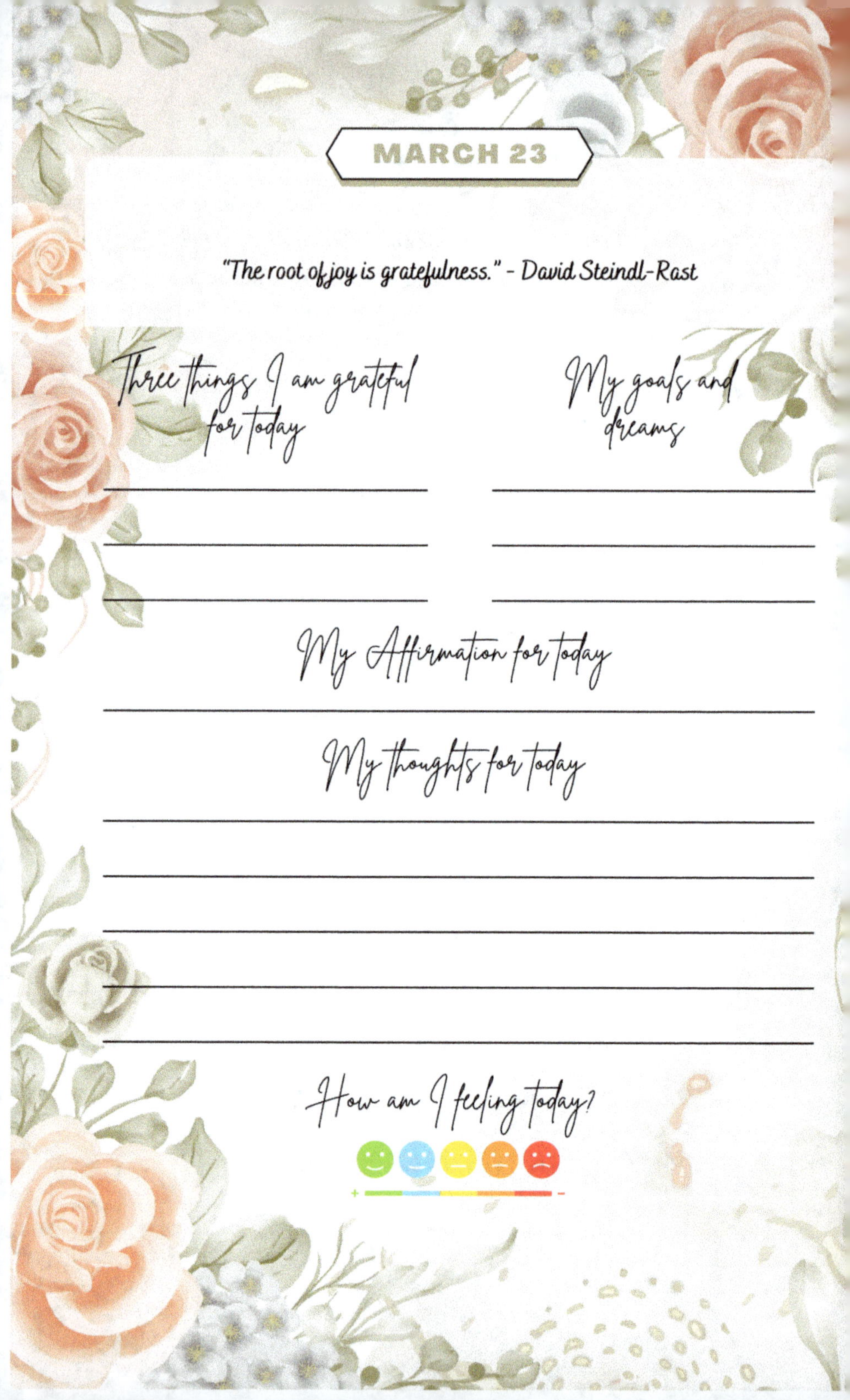

MARCH 23

"The root of joy is gratefulness." - David Steindl-Rast

Three things I am grateful for today

My goals and dreams

My Affirmation for today

My thoughts for today

How am I feeling today?

+ –

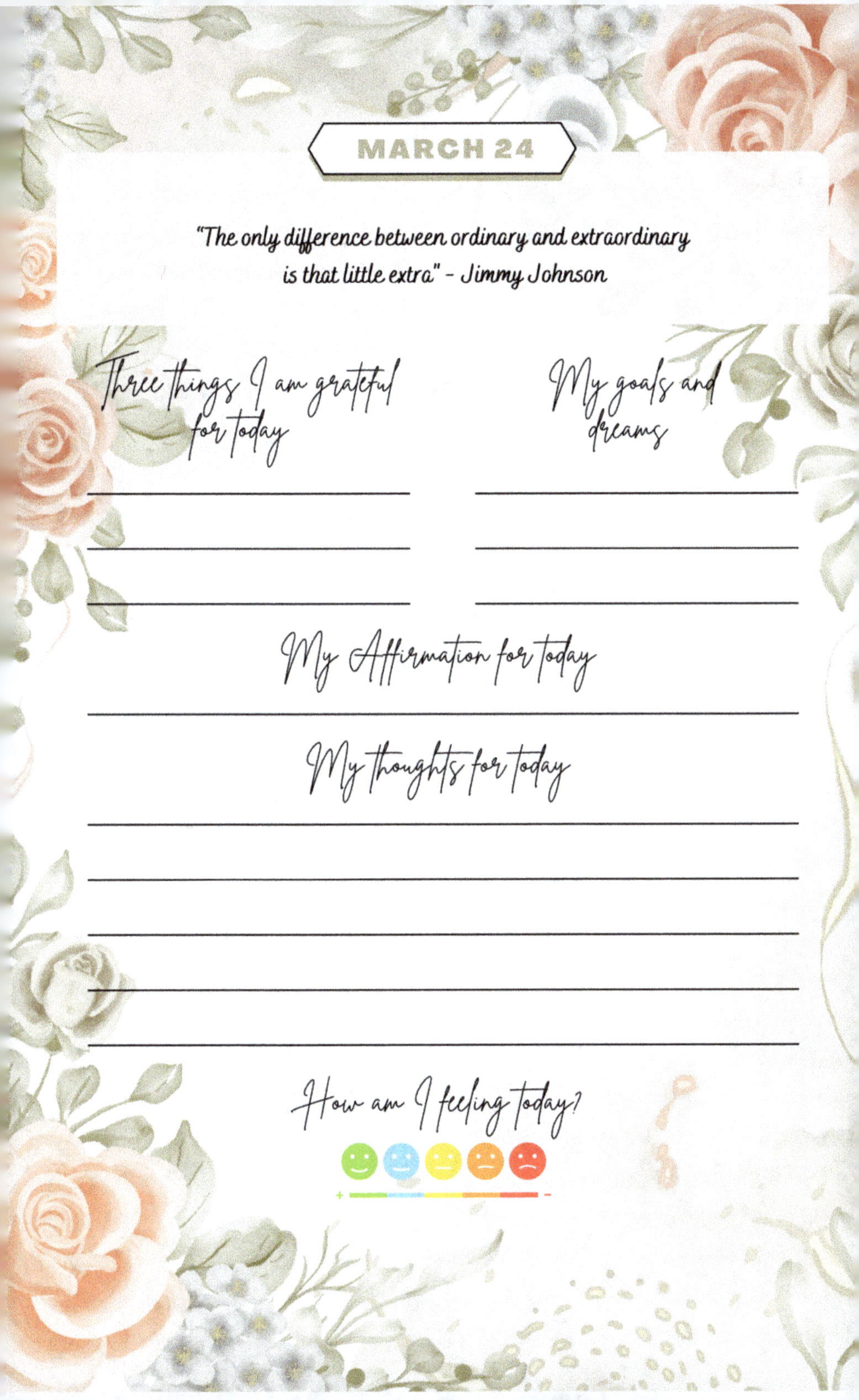

MARCH 24

"The only difference between ordinary and extraordinary is that little extra" - Jimmy Johnson

Three things I am grateful for today

My goals and dreams

My Affirmation for today

My thoughts for today

How am I feeling today?

+ −

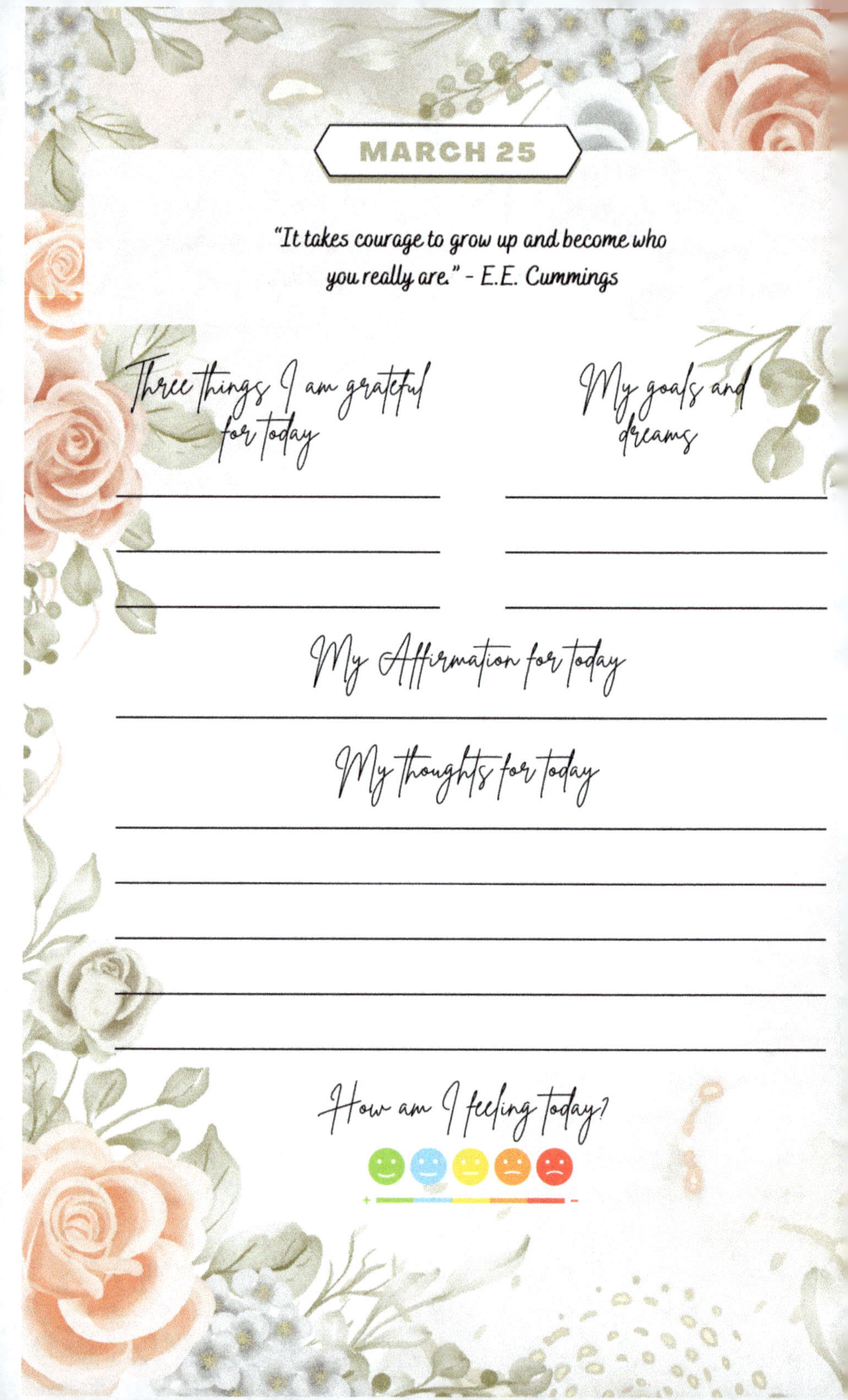

MARCH 25

"It takes courage to grow up and become who you really are." - E.E. Cummings

Three things I am grateful for today

My goals and dreams

My Affirmation for today

My thoughts for today

How am I feeling today?

+ –

MARCH 26

"Whatever you are, be a good one." - Abraham Lincoln

Three things I am grateful for today

My goals and dreams

My Affirmation for today

My thoughts for today

How am I feeling today?

MARCH 27

"Always be a first-rate version of yourself, instead of a second-rate version of somebody else." - Judy Garland

Three things I am grateful for today

My goals and dreams

My Affirmation for today

My thoughts for today

How am I feeling today?

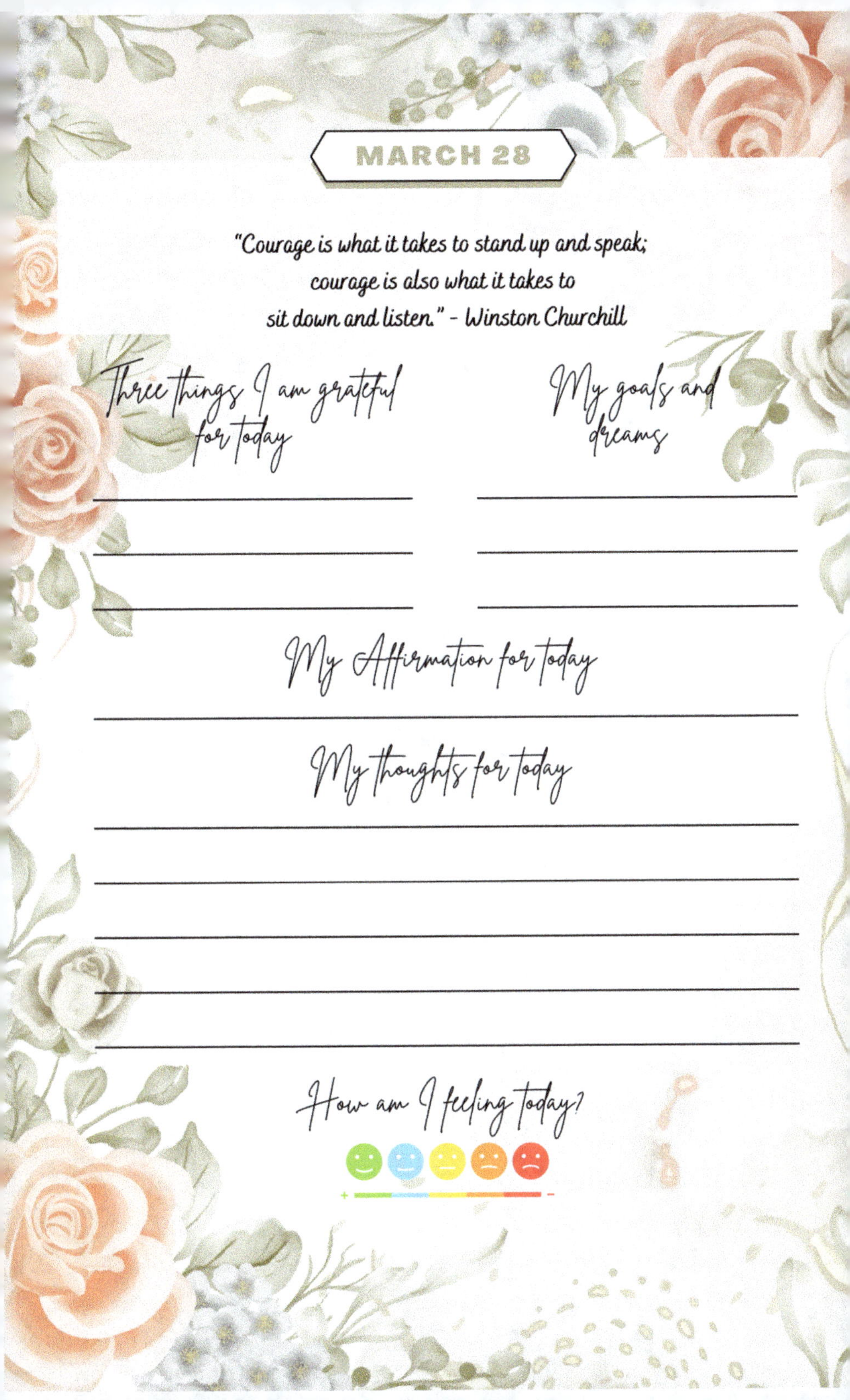

MARCH 28

"Courage is what it takes to stand up and speak; courage is also what it takes to sit down and listen." - Winston Churchill

Three things I am grateful for today

My goals and dreams

My Affirmation for today

My thoughts for today

How am I feeling today?

+ –

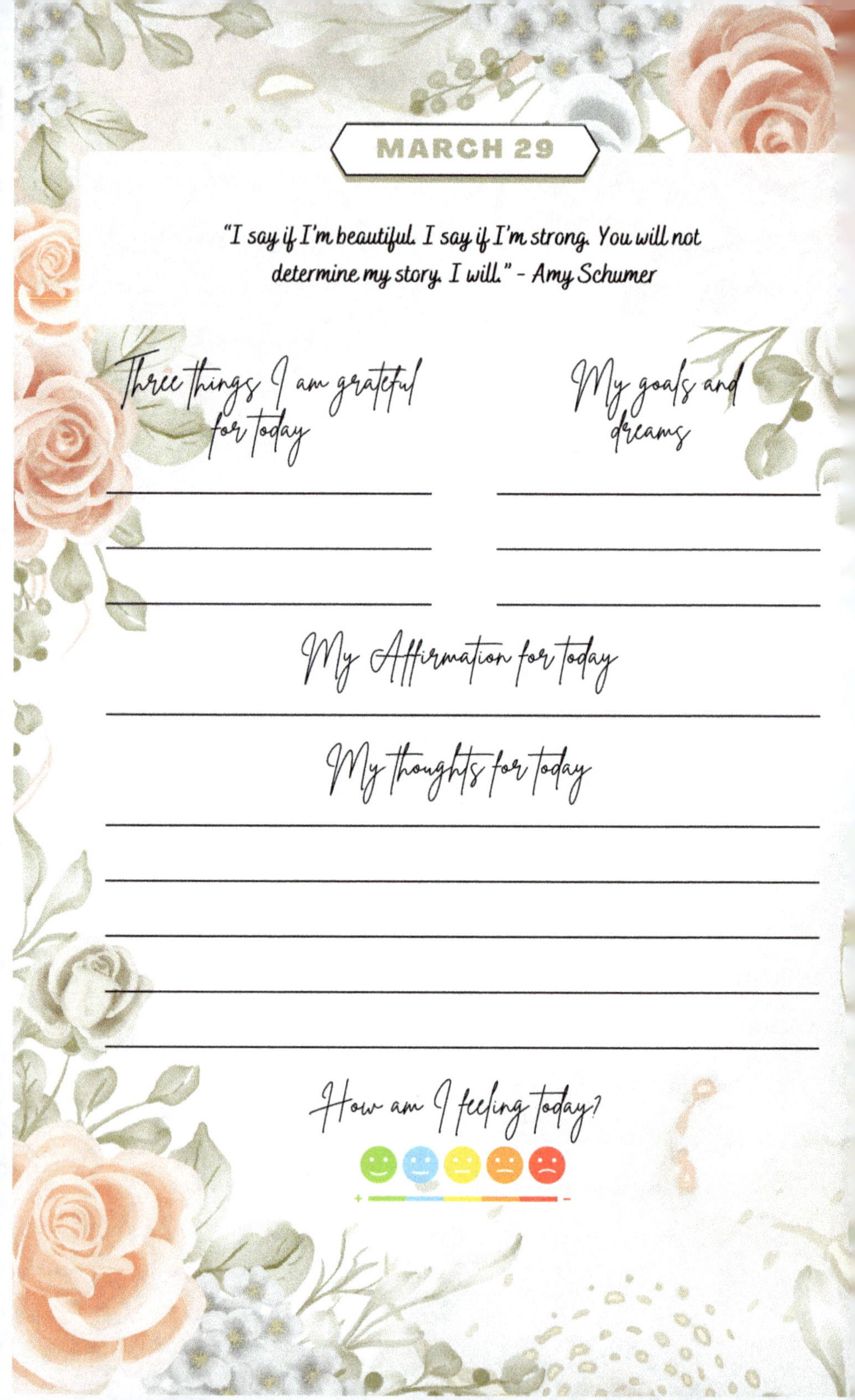

MARCH 29

"I say if I'm beautiful. I say if I'm strong. You will not determine my story. I will." - Amy Schumer

Three things I am grateful for today

My goals and dreams

My Affirmation for today

My thoughts for today

How am I feeling today?

+ −

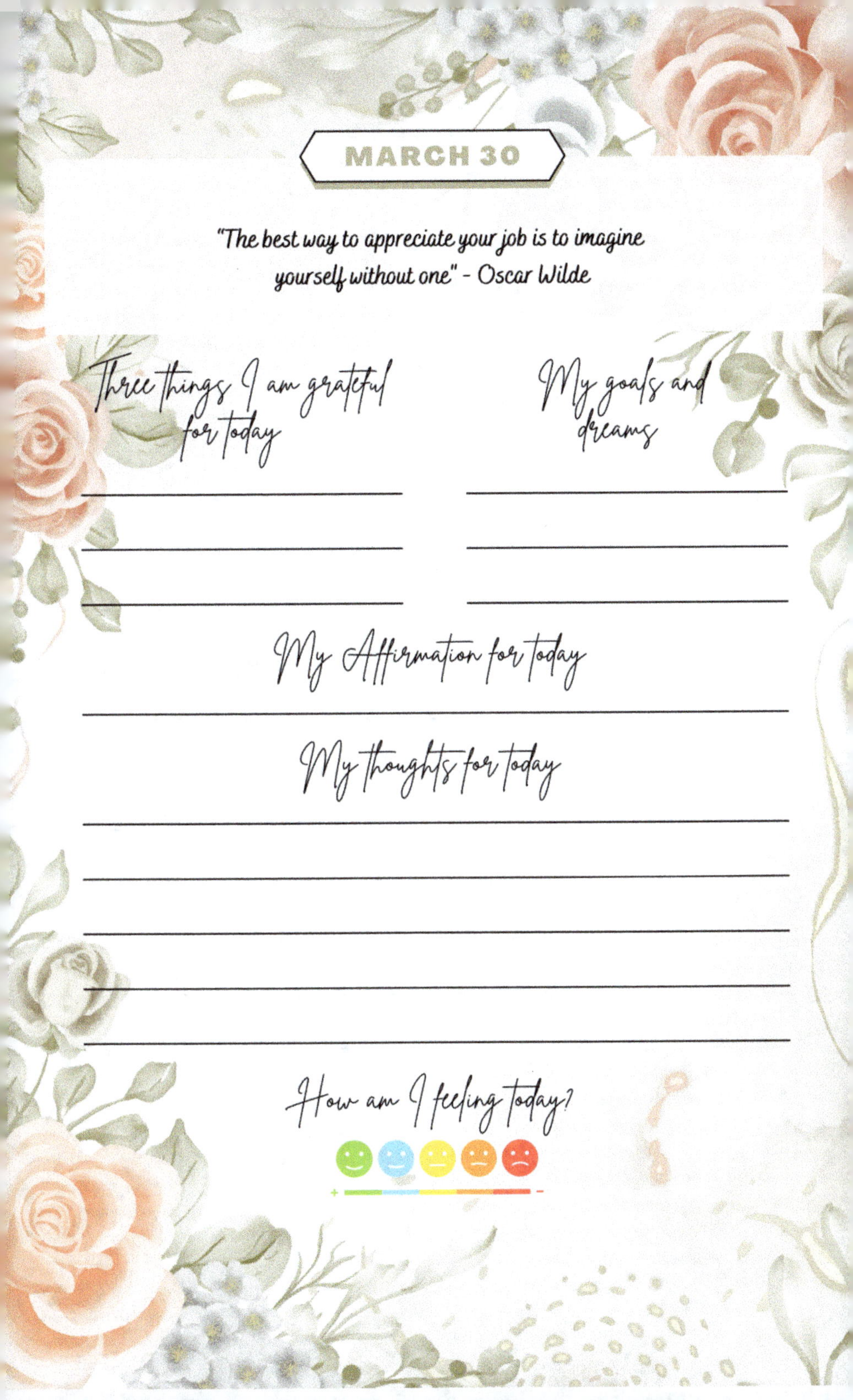

MARCH 30

"The best way to appreciate your job is to imagine yourself without one" - Oscar Wilde

Three things I am grateful for today

My goals and dreams

My Affirmation for today

My thoughts for today

How am I feeling today?

MARCH 31

"The secret to happiness is freedom ... and the secret to freedom is courage." - Thucydides

Three things I am grateful for today

My goals and dreams

My Affirmation for today

My thoughts for today

How am I feeling today?

+ –

APRIL 1

"When you are grateful, fear disappears and abundance appears" - Anthony Robbins

Three things I am grateful for today

My goals and dreams

My Affirmation for today

My thoughts for today

How am I feeling today?

\+ –

APRIL 2

"The question isn't who is going to let me; it's who is going to stop me?" - Ayn Rand

Three things I am grateful for today

My goals and dreams

My Affirmation for today

My thoughts for today

How am I feeling today?

APRIL 3

"The same boiling water that softens the potato hardens the egg. It's what you're made of. Not the circumstances." - Unknown

Three things I am grateful for today

My goals and dreams

My Affirmation for today

My thoughts for today

How am I feeling today?

+ −

APRIL 4

"Think like a queen. A queen is not afraid to fail. Failure is another stepping stone to greatness." - Oprah Winfrey

Three things I am grateful for today

____

____

____

My goals and dreams

____

____

____

My Affirmation for today

____

My thoughts for today

____

____

____

____

____

How am I feeling today?

\+ −

APRIL 5

"I cannot give you the formula for success, but I can give you the formula for failure, which is: Try to please everybody." - Herbert Swope

Three things I am grateful for today

My goals and dreams

My Affirmation for today

My thoughts for today

How am I feeling today?

\+ –

APRIL 6

"A wise girl knows her limits, a smart girl knows that she has none." - Marilyn Monroe

Three things I am grateful for today

My goals and dreams

My Affirmation for today

My thoughts for today

How am I feeling today?

+ –

APRIL 7

"You must always remember this: Have courage and be kind. You have more kindness in your little finger than most people possess in their whole body. And it has power. More than you know." - Brittany Candau

Three things I am grateful for today

My goals and dreams

My Affirmation for today

My thoughts for today

How am I feeling today?

APRIL 8

"Courage results when one's convictions are bigger than one's fears." - Orrin Woodward

Three things I am grateful for today

My goals and dreams

My Affirmation for today

My thoughts for today

How am I feeling today?

APRIL 9

"Winning means you're willing to go longer, work harder, and give more than anyone else" - Vince Lombardi

Three things I am grateful for today

My goals and dreams

My Affirmation for today

My thoughts for today

How am I feeling today?

APRIL 10

"The miracle is not that we do this work, but that we are happy to do it." - Mother Teresa

Three things I am grateful for today

My goals and dreams

My Affirmation for today

My thoughts for today

How am I feeling today?

\+ –

APRIL 11

"How do we change the world? One random act of kindness at a time." - Morgan Freeman

Three things I am grateful for today

____

____

____

My goals and dreams

____

____

____

My Affirmation for today

____

My thoughts for today

____

____

____

____

____

How am I feeling today?

\+ –

APRIL 12

"Courage is not the absence of fear but rather the assessment that something else is more important than fear." - Franklin D. Roosevelt

Three things I am grateful for today

My goals and dreams

My Affirmation for today

My thoughts for today

How am I feeling today?

\+ –

APRIL 13

"Impossible is just an opinion" - Paulo Coelho

Three things I am grateful for today

My goals and dreams

My Affirmation for today

My thoughts for today

How am I feeling today?

+ −

APRIL 14

"Never give up on a dream just because of the time it will take to accomplish it. The time will pass anyway." - Earl Nightingale

Three things I am grateful for today

My goals and dreams

My Affirmation for today

My thoughts for today

How am I feeling today?

APRIL 15

"When I was young, I admired clever people. Now that I am old, I admire kind people." - Abraham Joshua Heschel

Three things I am grateful for today

My goals and dreams

My Affirmation for today

My thoughts for today

How am I feeling today?

+ -

APRIL 16

"If you work on something a little bit every day, you end up with something that is massive." - Kenneth Goldsmith

Three things I am grateful for today

My goals and dreams

My Affirmation for today

My thoughts for today

How am I feeling today?

+ −

APRIL 17

"If we have the attitude that it's going to be a great day it usually is." - Catherine Pulsifier

Three things I am grateful for today

____

____

____

My goals and dreams

____

____

____

My Affirmation for today

____

My thoughts for today

____

____

____

____

____

How am I feeling today?

\+ –

APRIL 18

"The big secret in life is that there is no secret. Whatever your goal, you can get there if you're willing to work." - Oprah Winfrey

Three things I am grateful for today

____
____
____

My goals and dreams

____
____
____

My Affirmation for today

____

My thoughts for today

____
____
____
____
____

How am I feeling today?

APRIL 19

"A girl should be two things: who and what she wants." - Coco Chanel

Three things I am grateful for today

My goals and dreams

My Affirmation for today

My thoughts for today

How am I feeling today?

APRIL 20

"Be the person your dog thinks you are." - Ricky Gervais

Three things I am grateful for today

My goals and dreams

My Affirmation for today

My thoughts for today

How am I feeling today?

APRIL 21

"Imperfection is beauty, madness is genius and it's better to be absolutely ridiculous than absolutely boring." - Marilyn Monroe

Three things I am grateful for today

My goals and dreams

My Affirmation for today

My thoughts for today

How am I feeling today?

\+ –

APRIL 22

"Don't stop when you are tired. Stop when you are done" - Unknown

Three things I am grateful for today

My goals and dreams

My Affirmation for today

My thoughts for today

How am I feeling today?

\+ –

APRIL 23

"It's the possibility of having a dream come true that makes life interesting" - Paulo Coelho

Three things I am grateful for today

___

___

___

My goals and dreams

___

___

___

My Affirmation for today

___

My thoughts for today

___

___

___

___

___

How am I feeling today?

\+ −

APRIL 24

"Be who you are and say what you feel, because those who mind don't matter, and those who matter don't mind." - Bernard M. Maruch

Three things I am grateful for today

My goals and dreams

My Affirmation for today

My thoughts for today

How am I feeling today?

APRIL 25

"If you cannot do great things, do small things in a great way." - Napoleon Hill

Three things I am grateful for today

My goals and dreams

My Affirmation for today

My thoughts for today

How am I feeling today?

\+ –

APRIL 26

"Be yourself; everyone else is already taken." - Oscar Wilde

Three things I am grateful for today

My goals and dreams

My Affirmation for today

My thoughts for today

How am I feeling today?

APRIL 27

"When I was a child my mother said to me, 'If you become a soldier, you'll be a general. If you become a monk, you'll be the pope.' Instead I became a painter and wound up as Picasso" - Picasso

Three things I am grateful for today

My goals and dreams

My Affirmation for today

My thoughts for today

How am I feeling today?

APRIL 28

"Compliment people wherever you go. Praise every single thing you see. Be a ray of sunshine to everyone you meet." - Rhonda Byrne

Three things I am grateful for today

My goals and dreams

My Affirmation for today

My thoughts for today

How am I feeling today?

\+ –

APRIL 29

"At any given moment you have the power to say: this is not how the story is going to end." - Unknown

Three things I am grateful for today

My goals and dreams

My Affirmation for today

My thoughts for today

How am I feeling today?

\+ –

APRIL 30

"Alone time is when I distance myself from the voices of the world so I can hear my own" - Oprah Winfrey

Three things I am grateful for today

My goals and dreams

My Affirmation for today

My thoughts for today

How am I feeling today?

MAY 1

"Don't limit your challenges. Challenge your limits." - Unknown

Three things I am grateful for today

My goals and dreams

My Affirmation for today

My thoughts for today

How am I feeling today?

MAY 2

"To be beautiful means to be yourself. You don't need to be accepted by others. You need to accept yourself." - Bindi Irwin

Three things I am grateful for today

My goals and dreams

My Affirmation for today

My thoughts for today

How am I feeling today?

MAY 3

"Whenever you find yourself doubting how far you can go, just remember how far you have come." - Unknown

Three things I am grateful for today

My goals and dreams

My Affirmation for today

My thoughts for today

How am I feeling today?

MAY 4

"If you hear a voice within you say, 'You cannot paint,' then by all means paint, and that voice will be silenced." - Vincent Van Gogh

Three things I am grateful for today

My goals and dreams

My Affirmation for today

My thoughts for today

How am I feeling today?

MAY 5

"Most importantly, keep smiling. Because life is a beautiful thing and there's so much to smile about." - Marilyn Monroe

Three things I am grateful for today

My goals and dreams

My Affirmation for today

My thoughts for today

How am I feeling today?

MAY 6

"Good. Better. Best. Never let it rest.
'Til your good is better and
your better is best." - St. Jerome.

Three things I am grateful for today

My goals and dreams

My Affirmation for today

My thoughts for today

How am I feeling today?

MAY 7

"A woman is the full circle. Within her is
the power to create,
nurture and transform." - Diane Mariechild

Three things I am grateful for today

My goals and dreams

My Affirmation for today

My thoughts for today

How am I feeling today?

\+ −

MAY 8

"In the middle of every difficulty lies opportunity." - Albert Einstein

Three things I am grateful for today

My goals and dreams

My Affirmation for today

My thoughts for today

How am I feeling today?

\+ –

"The best of times is now." - Oprah Winfrey

Three things I am grateful for today

My goals and dreams

My Affirmation for today

My thoughts for today

How am I feeling today?

\+ –

MAY 10

"Start where you are. Use what you have. Do what you can." - Arthur Ashe

Three things I am grateful for today

My goals and dreams

My Affirmation for today

My thoughts for today

How am I feeling today?

\+ –

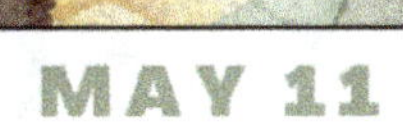

MAY 11

"Dreams don't work unless you do."
- John C. Maxwell

Three things I am grateful for today

My goals and dreams

My Affirmation for today

My thoughts for today

How am I feeling today?

\+ –

MAY 12

"Go the extra mile. It's never crowded there."
- Dr. Wayne D. Dyer

Three things I am grateful for today

My goals and dreams

My Affirmation for today

My thoughts for today

How am I feeling today?

MAY 13

"Hustle in silence and let your success make the noise." - Unknown

Three things I am grateful for today

My goals and dreams

My Affirmation for today

My thoughts for today

How am I feeling today?

MAY 14

"We cannot solve our problems with the same thinking we used when we created them" - Albert Einstein

Three things I am grateful for today

My goals and dreams

My Affirmation for today

My thoughts for today

How am I feeling today?

MAY 15

"The secret of your future is hidden in your daily routine." - Mike Murdock

Three things I am grateful for today

My goals and dreams

My Affirmation for today

My thoughts for today

How am I feeling today?

+ –

MAY 16

"Keep your face always toward the sunshine—and shadows will fall behind you." - Walt Whitman

Three things I am grateful for today

My goals and dreams

My Affirmation for today

My thoughts for today

How am I feeling today?

\+ –

MAY 17

"What defines us is how well we rise after falling."

- Lionel from the movie Maid in Manhattan

Three things I am grateful for today

My goals and dreams

My Affirmation for today

My thoughts for today

How am I feeling today?

MAY 18

"Make each day your masterpiece."
- John Wooden

Three things I am grateful for today

My goals and dreams

My Affirmation for today

My thoughts for today

How am I feeling today?

MAY 19

"We must reject not only the stereotypes
that others hold of us,
but also the stereotypes that we
hold of ourselves." - Shirley Chisholm

Three things I am grateful for today

My goals and dreams

My Affirmation for today

My thoughts for today

How am I feeling today?

MAY 20

"Wherever you go, go with all your heart."

- Confucius

Three things I am grateful for today

My goals and dreams

My Affirmation for today

My thoughts for today

How am I feeling today?

MAY 21

"Love, because when you love, you are using the greatest power in the Universe." - Rhonda Byrne

Three things I am grateful for today

My goals and dreams

My Affirmation for today

My thoughts for today

How am I feeling today?

\+ −

MAY 22

"Turn your wounds into wisdom." - Oprah Winfrey

Three things I am grateful for today

My goals and dreams

My Affirmation for today

My thoughts for today

How am I feeling today?

MAY 23

"We can do anything we want to if we stick to it long enough."- Helen Keller

Three things I am grateful for today

My goals and dreams

My Affirmation for today

My thoughts for today

How am I feeling today?

\+ –

MAY 24

"Success is no accident. It is hard work, perseverance, learning, studying, sacrifice and most of all, love of what you are doing or learning to do."- Pele

Three things I am grateful for today

My goals and dreams

My Affirmation for today

My thoughts for today

How am I feeling today?

MAY 25

"There is no limit to what we, as women, can accomplish." - Michelle Obama

Three things I am grateful for today

My goals and dreams

My Affirmation for today

My thoughts for today

How am I feeling today?

\+ −

MAY 26

"Not in doing what you like, but in liking what you do is the secret of happiness." - J.M. Barrie

Three things I am grateful for today

My goals and dreams

My Affirmation for today

My thoughts for today

How am I feeling today?

"Joy is the simplest form of gratitude."
- Karl Barth

Three things I am grateful for today

My goals and dreams

My Affirmation for today

My thoughts for today

How am I feeling today?

MAY 28

"Every champion was once a contender that didn't give up." - Gabby Douglas

Three things I am grateful for today

My goals and dreams

My Affirmation for today

My thoughts for today

How am I feeling today?

\+ −

"Be thankful for what you have; you'll end up having more. If you concentrate on what you don't have, you will never, ever have enough."

- Oprah Winfrey

Three things I am grateful for today

My goals and dreams

My Affirmation for today

My thoughts for today

How am I feeling today?

MAY 30

"Be kind whenever possible. It is always possible." - The 14th Dalai Lama

Three things I am grateful for today

My goals and dreams

My Affirmation for today

My thoughts for today

How am I feeling today?

\+ −

MAY 31

"My father gave me the best advice of my life. He said, 'Whatever you do, don't wake up at 65 years old and think about what you should have done with your life.'" - George Clooney

Three things I am grateful for today

My goals and dreams

My Affirmation for today

My thoughts for today

How am I feeling today?

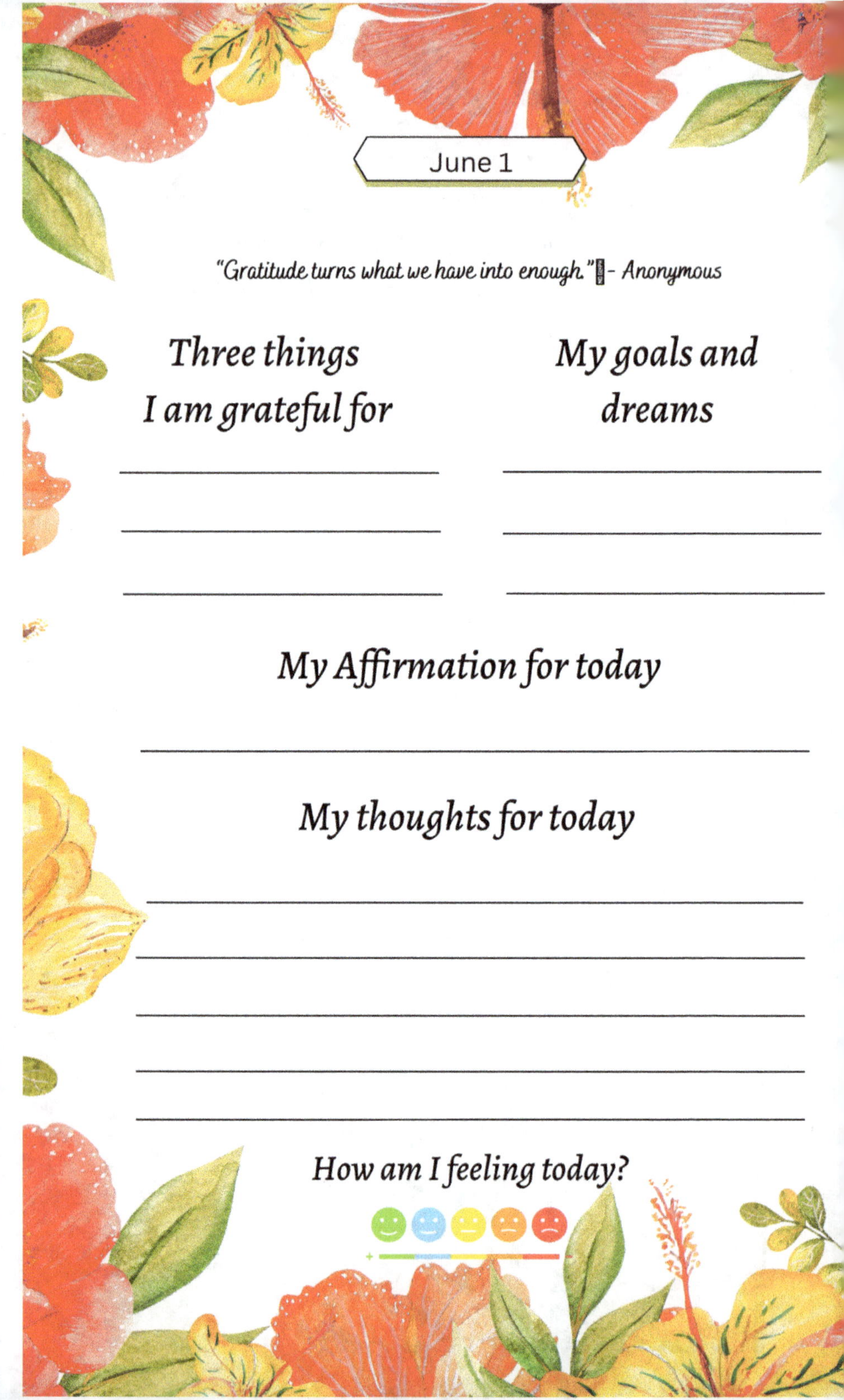

June 1

"Gratitude turns what we have into enough." - Anonymous

Three things I am grateful for

____

____

____

My goals and dreams

____

____

____

My Affirmation for today

____

My thoughts for today

____

____

____

____

____

How am I feeling today?

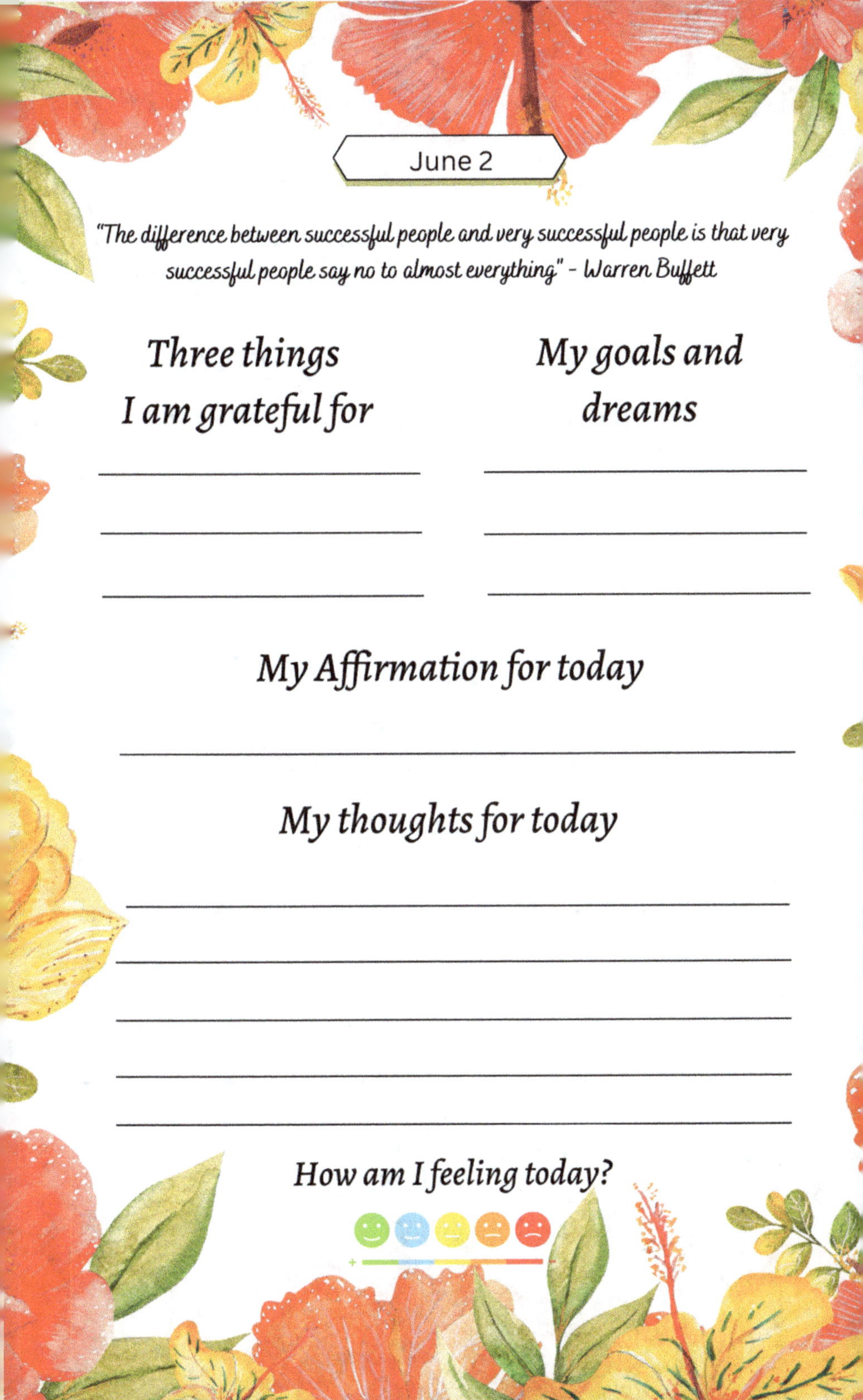

June 2

"The difference between successful people and very successful people is that very successful people say no to almost everything" - Warren Buffett

Three things I am grateful for

My goals and dreams

My Affirmation for today

My thoughts for today

How am I feeling today?

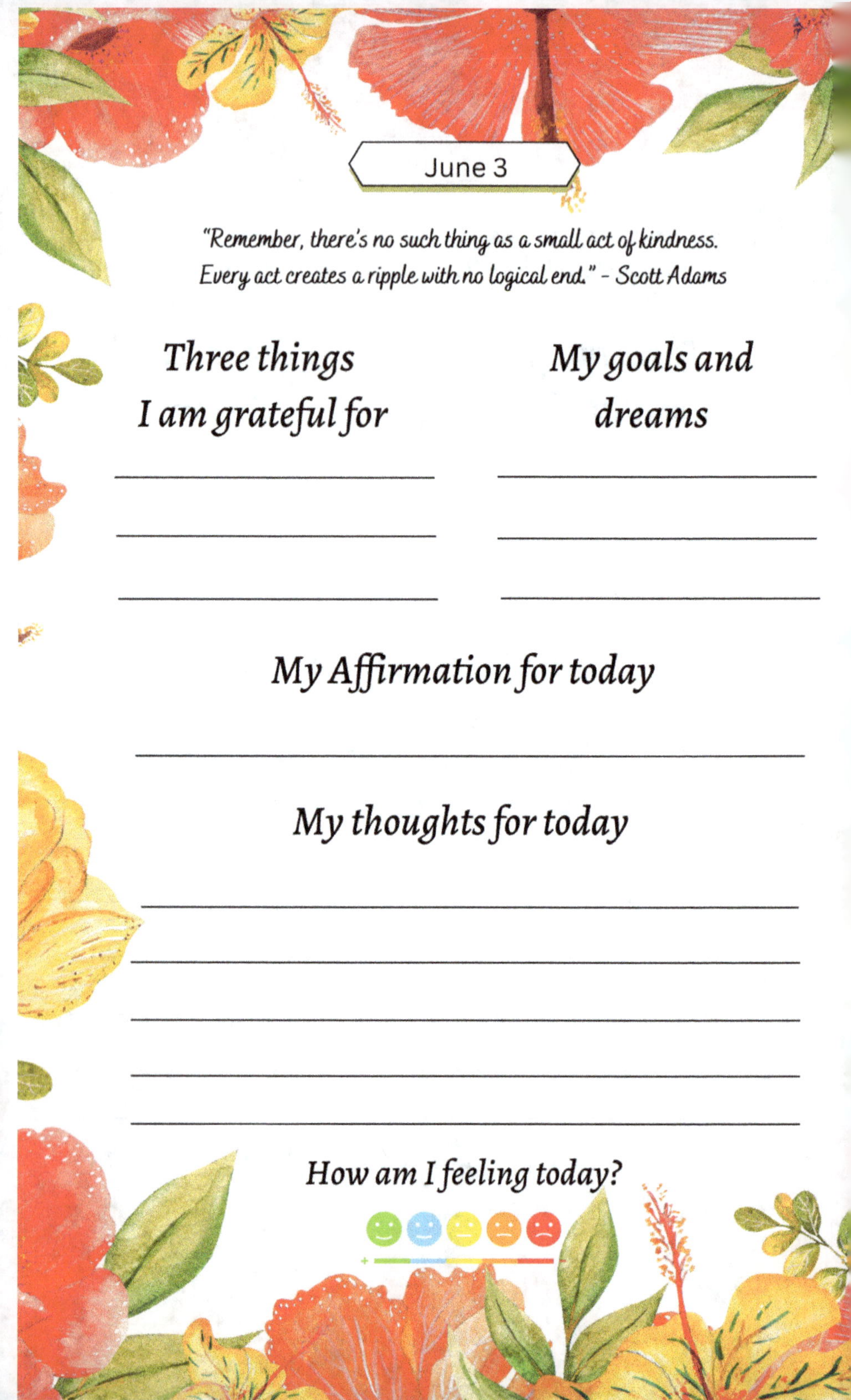

June 3

"Remember, there's no such thing as a small act of kindness. Every act creates a ripple with no logical end." - Scott Adams

Three things I am grateful for

My goals and dreams

My Affirmation for today

My thoughts for today

How am I feeling today?

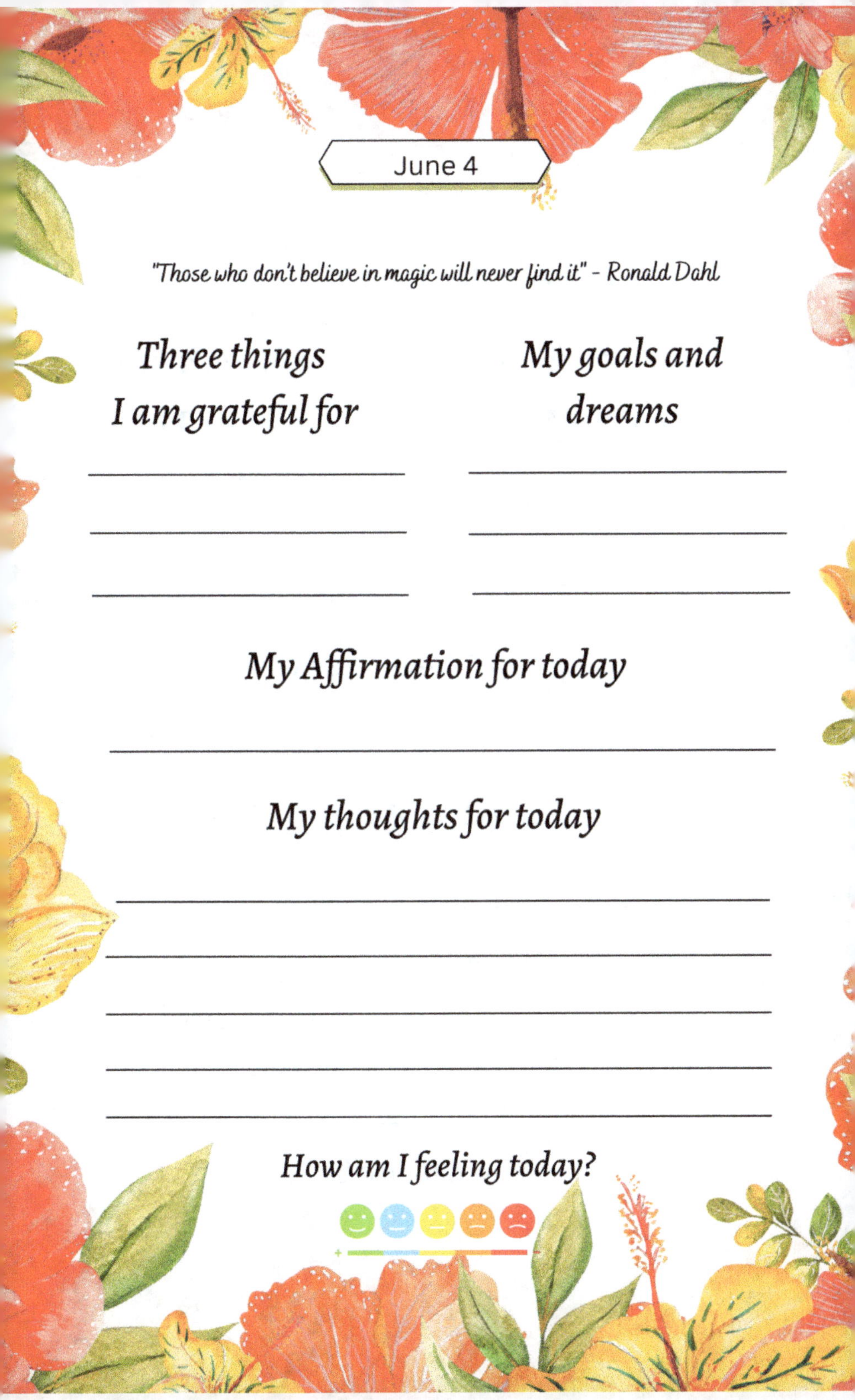

June 4

"Those who don't believe in magic will never find it" - Ronald Dahl

Three things I am grateful for

My goals and dreams

My Affirmation for today

My thoughts for today

How am I feeling today?

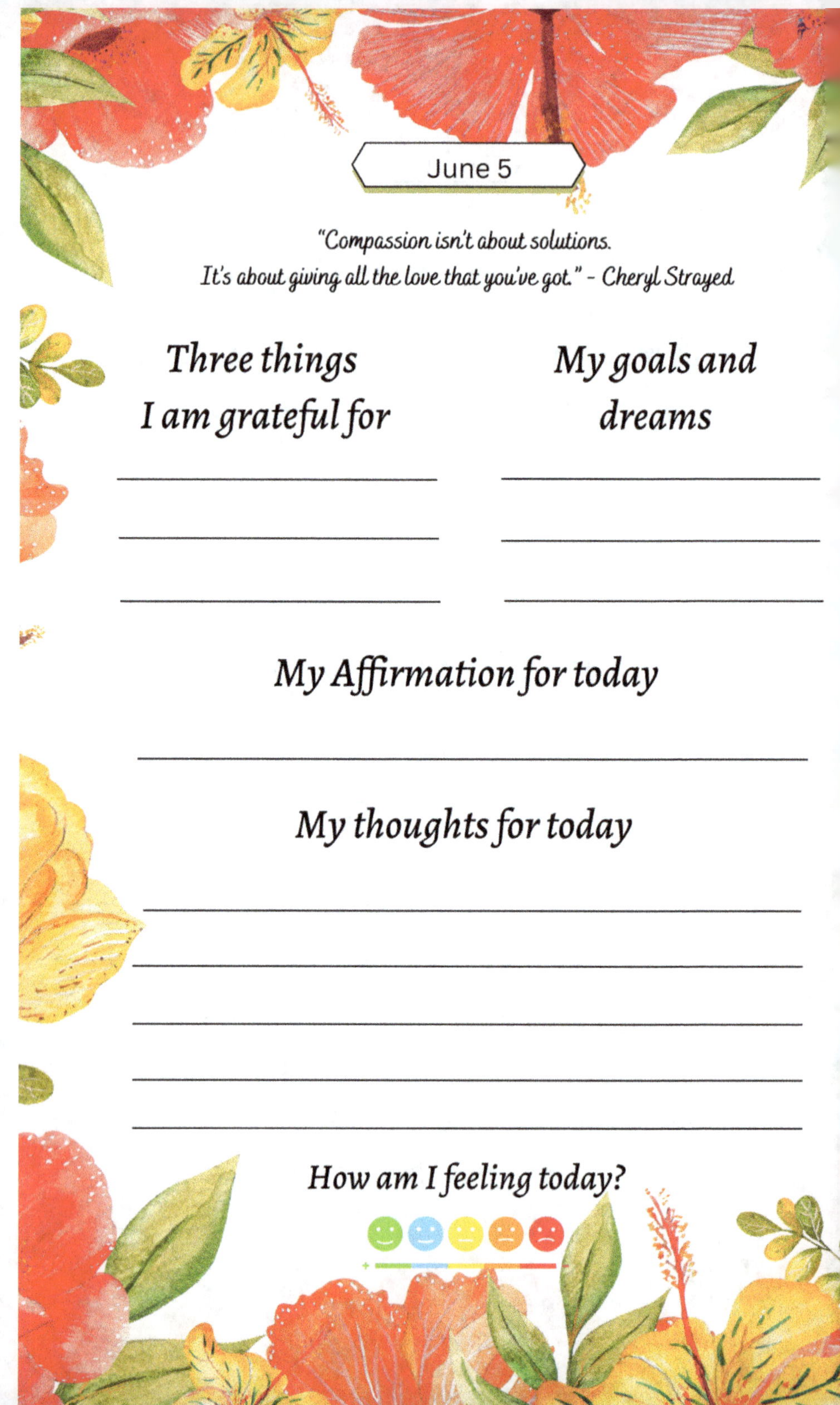

June 5

"Compassion isn't about solutions.
It's about giving all the love that you've got." - Cheryl Strayed

Three things I am grateful for

My goals and dreams

My Affirmation for today

My thoughts for today

How am I feeling today?

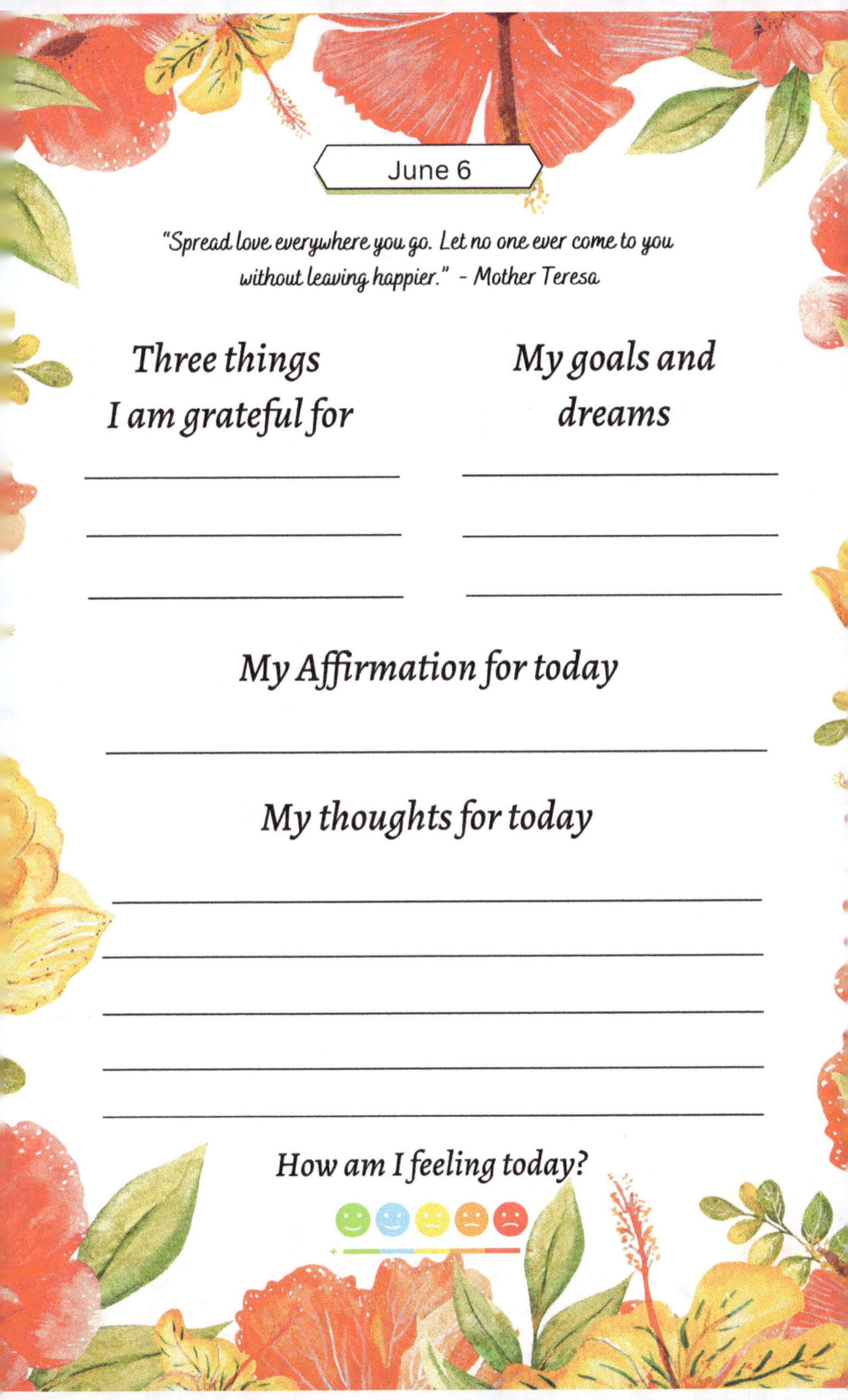

June 6

"Spread love everywhere you go. Let no one ever come to you without leaving happier." - Mother Teresa

Three things I am grateful for

My goals and dreams

My Affirmation for today

My thoughts for today

How am I feeling today?

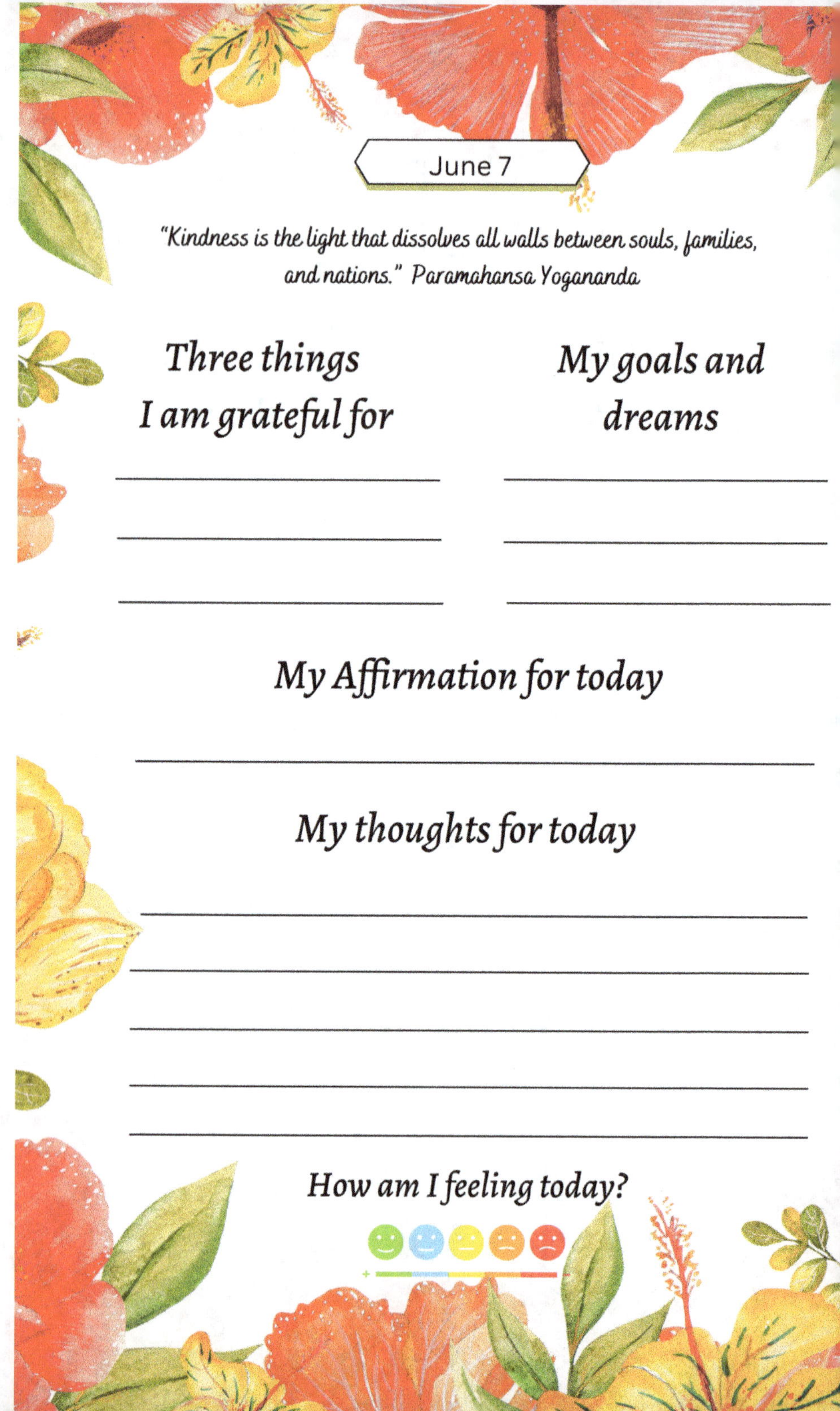

June 7

"Kindness is the light that dissolves all walls between souls, families, and nations." Paramahansa Yogananda

Three things I am grateful for

My goals and dreams

My Affirmation for today

My thoughts for today

How am I feeling today?

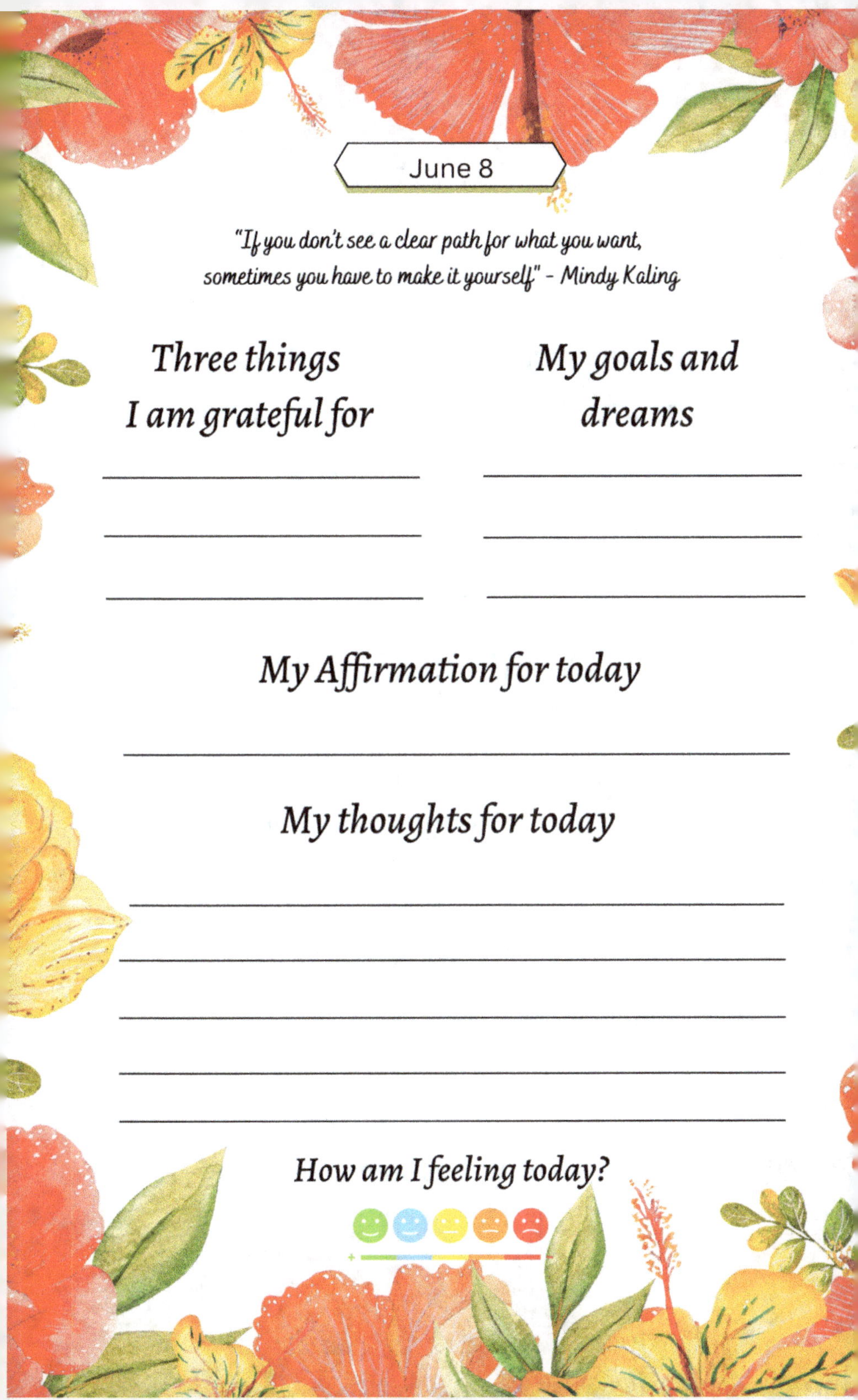

June 8

"If you don't see a clear path for what you want, sometimes you have to make it yourself" - Mindy Kaling

Three things I am grateful for	My goals and dreams
____________	____________
____________	____________
____________	____________

My Affirmation for today

____

My thoughts for today

____

____

____

____

____

How am I feeling today?

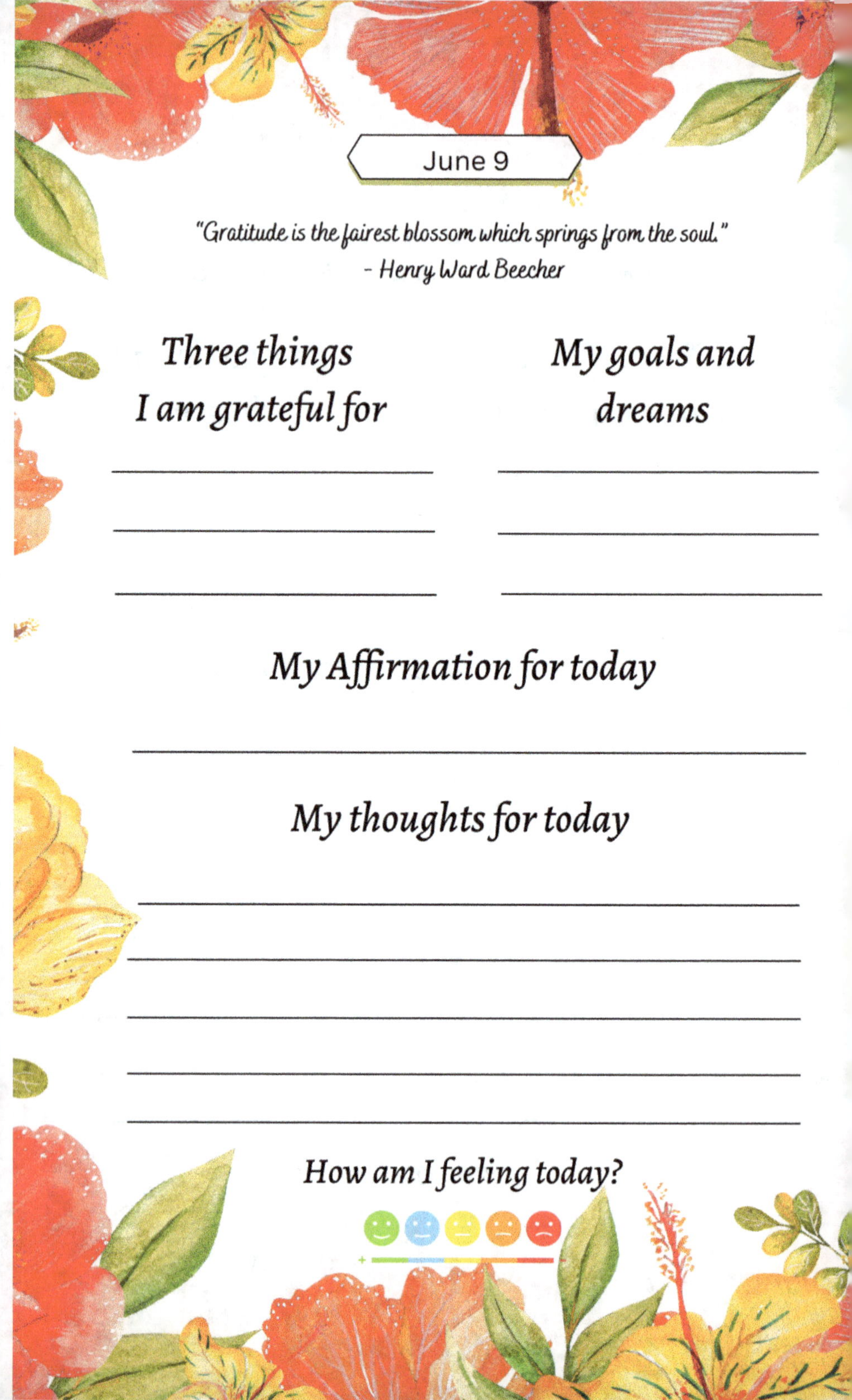

June 9

"Gratitude is the fairest blossom which springs from the soul."
- Henry Ward Beecher

Three things I am grateful for

My goals and dreams

My Affirmation for today

My thoughts for today

How am I feeling today?

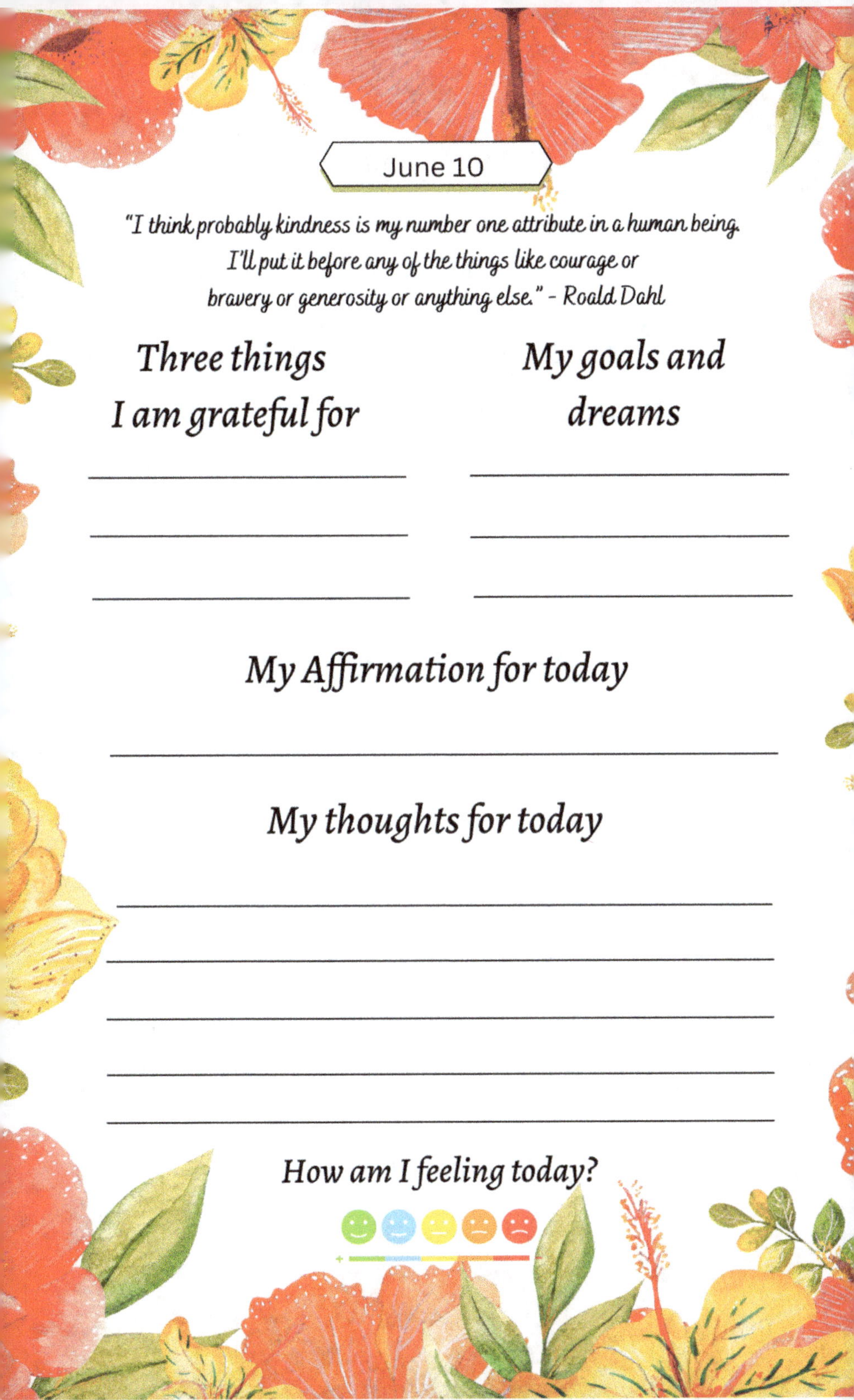

June 10

"I think probably kindness is my number one attribute in a human being. I'll put it before any of the things like courage or bravery or generosity or anything else." - Roald Dahl

Three things I am grateful for

____

____

____

My goals and dreams

____

____

____

My Affirmation for today

____

My thoughts for today

____

____

____

____

____

How am I feeling today?

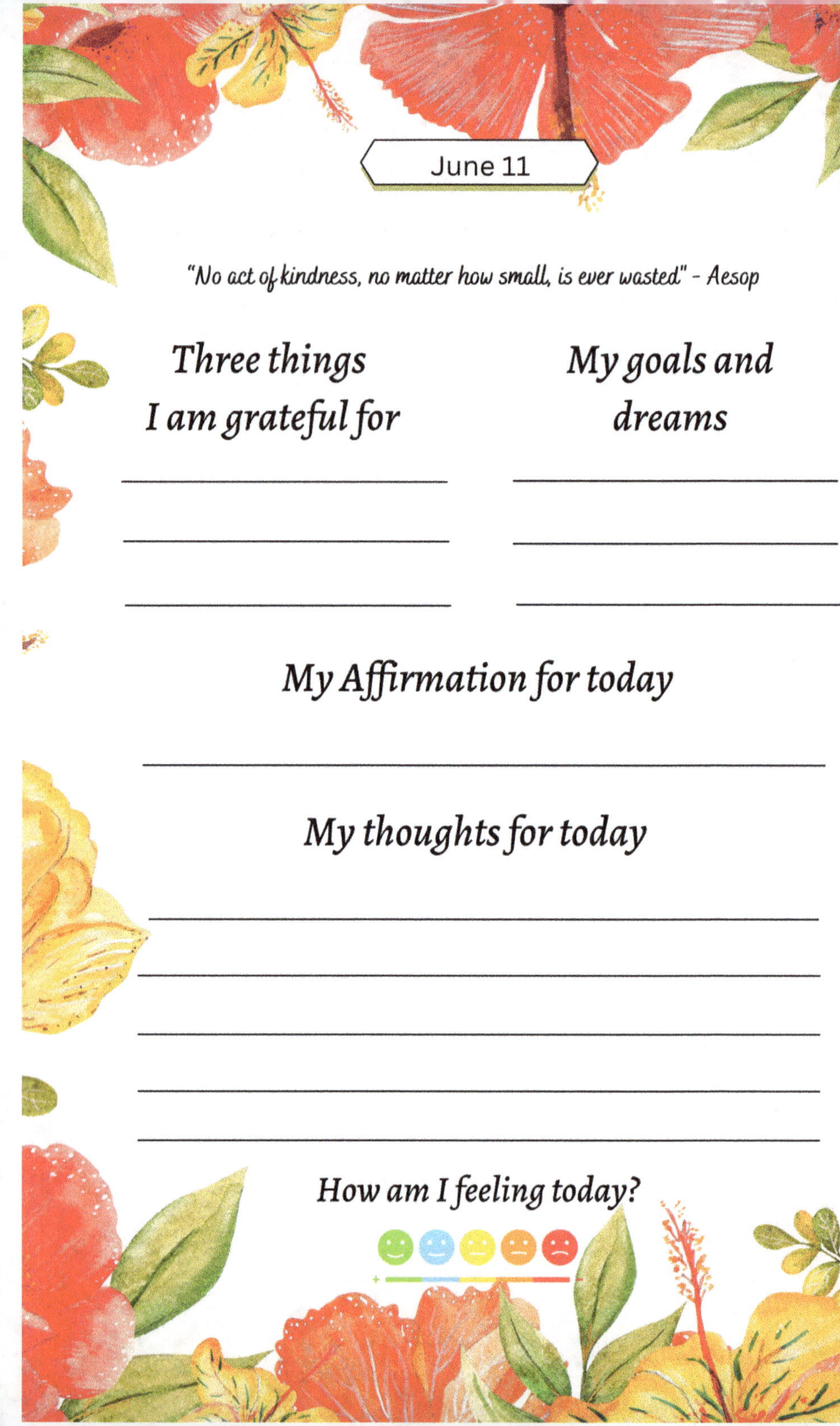

June 11

"No act of kindness, no matter how small, is ever wasted" - Aesop

Three things I am grateful for

My goals and dreams

My Affirmation for today

My thoughts for today

How am I feeling today?

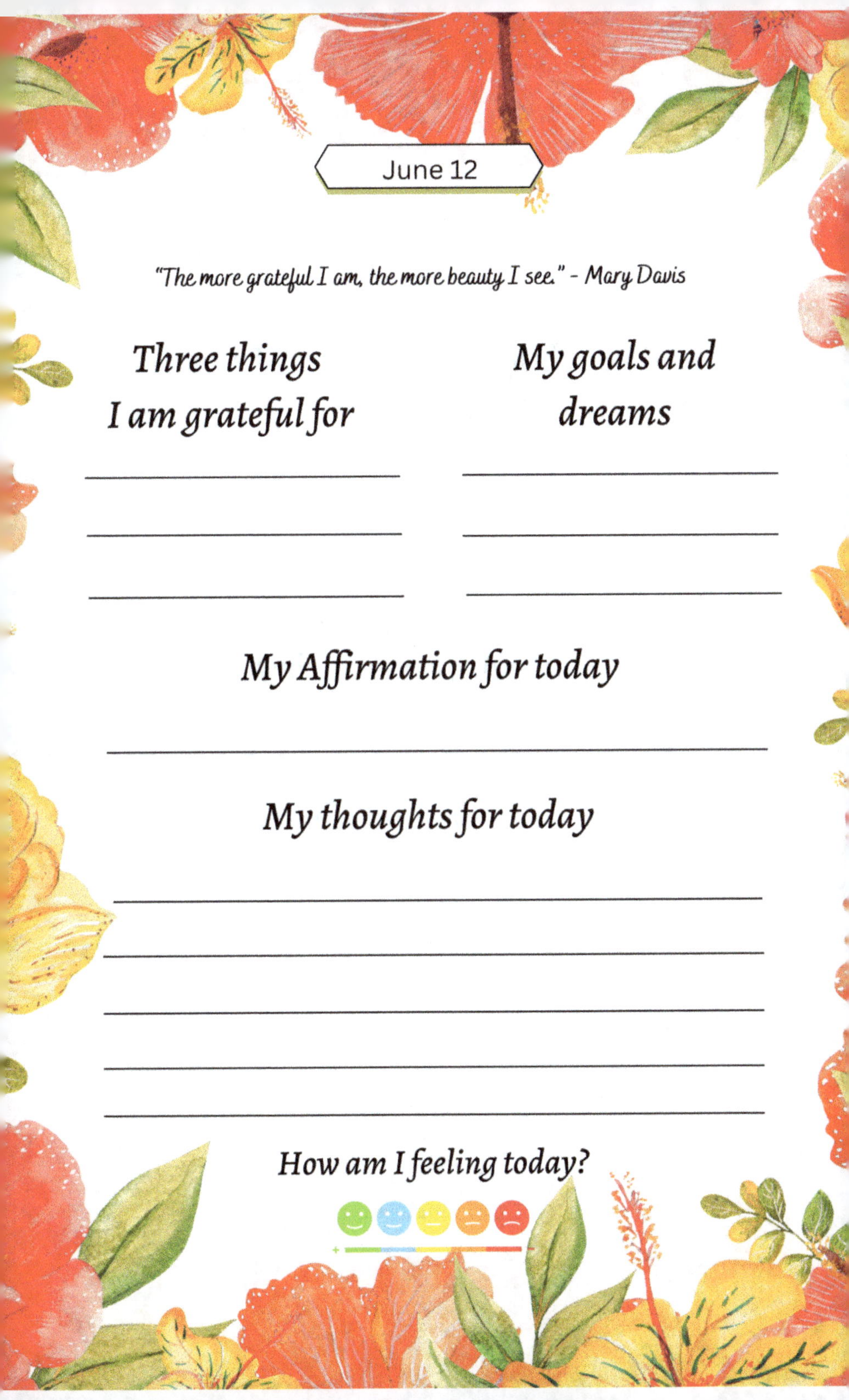

June 12

"The more grateful I am, the more beauty I see." - Mary Davis

Three things I am grateful for

My goals and dreams

My Affirmation for today

My thoughts for today

How am I feeling today?

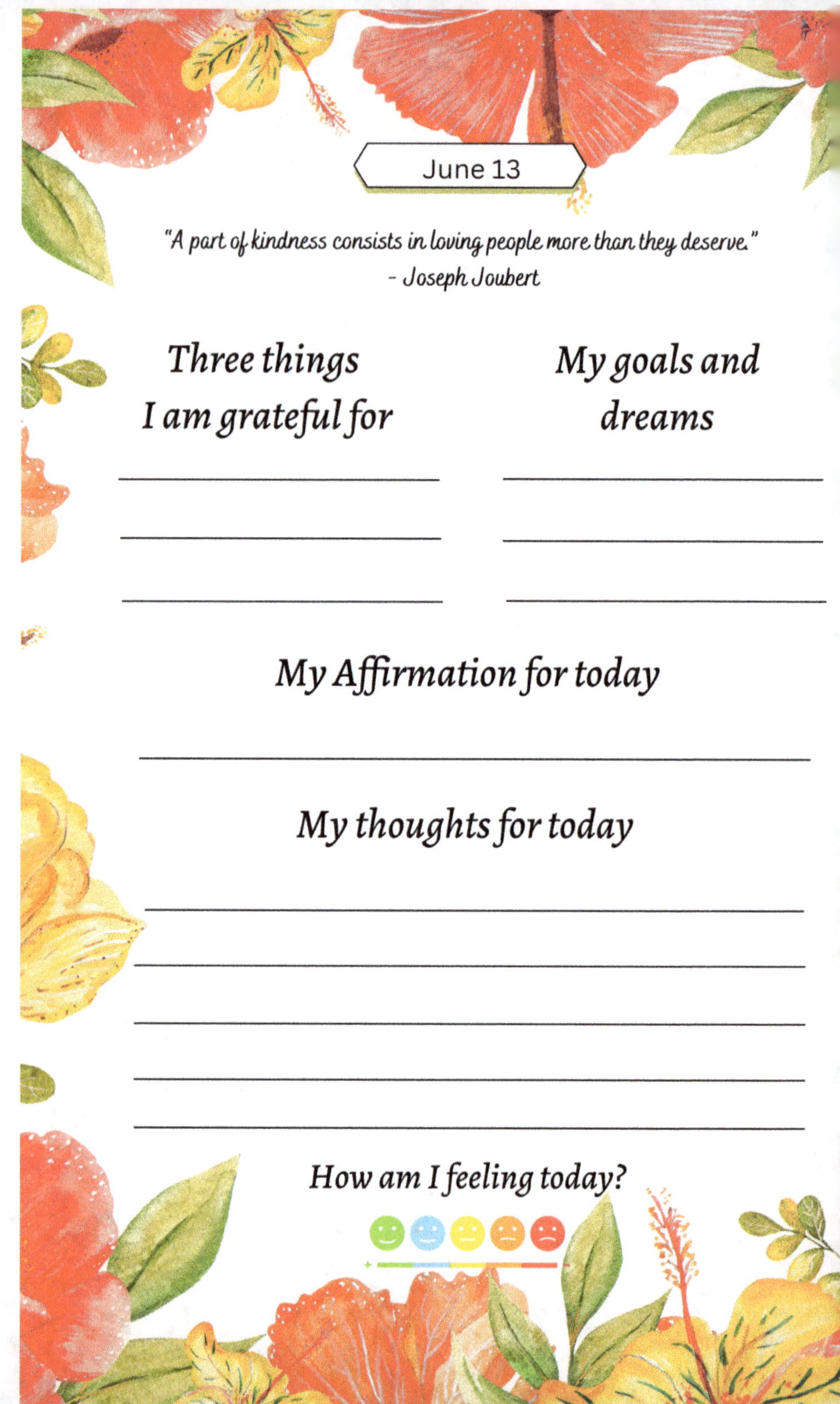

June 13

"A part of kindness consists in loving people more than they deserve."
- Joseph Joubert

Three things I am grateful for

____

____

____

My goals and dreams

____

____

____

My Affirmation for today

____

My thoughts for today

____

____

____

____

____

How am I feeling today?

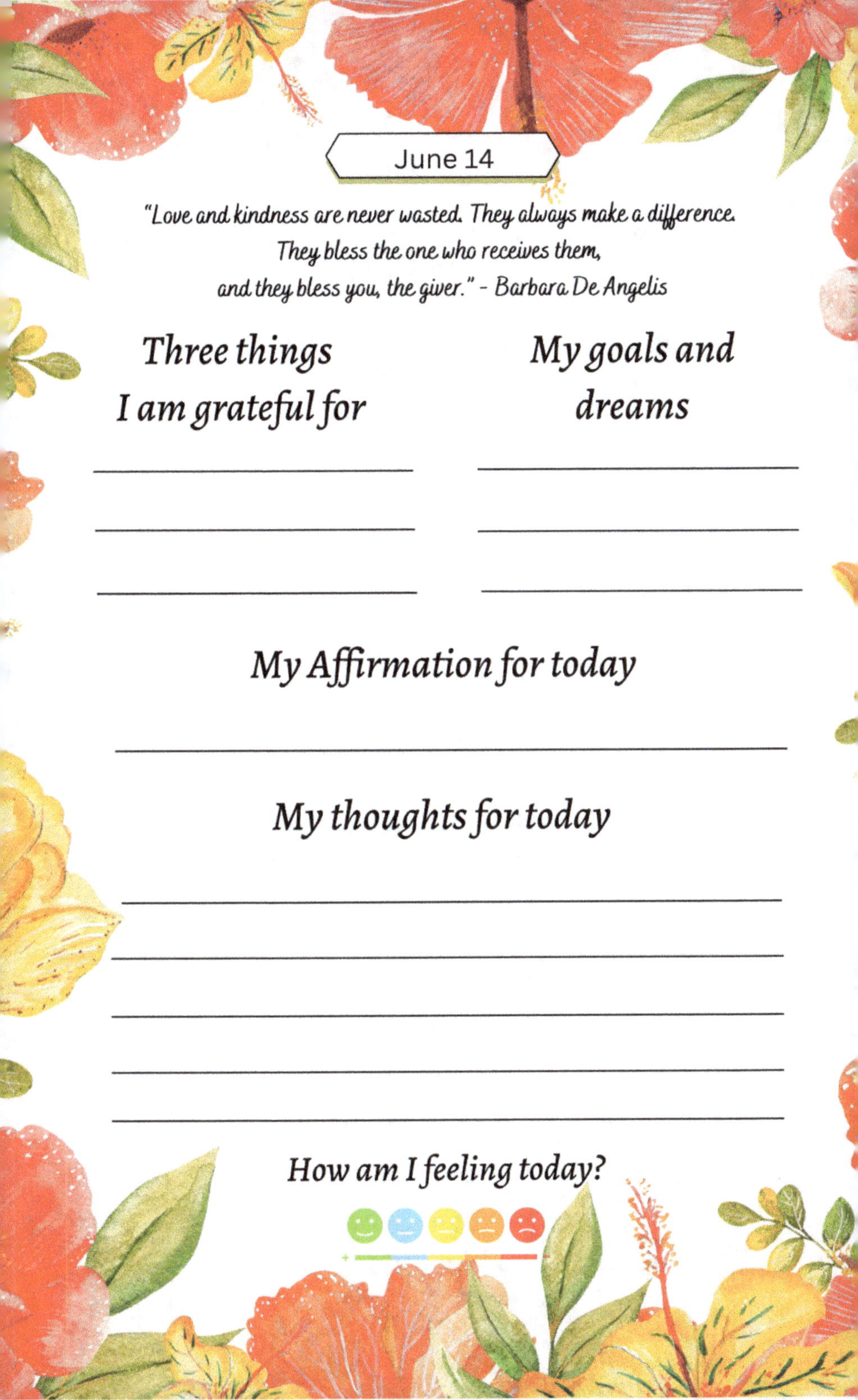

June 14

"Love and kindness are never wasted. They always make a difference. They bless the one who receives them, and they bless you, the giver." - Barbara De Angelis

Three things I am grateful for

____

____

____

My goals and dreams

____

____

____

My Affirmation for today

____

My thoughts for today

____

____

____

____

____

How am I feeling today?

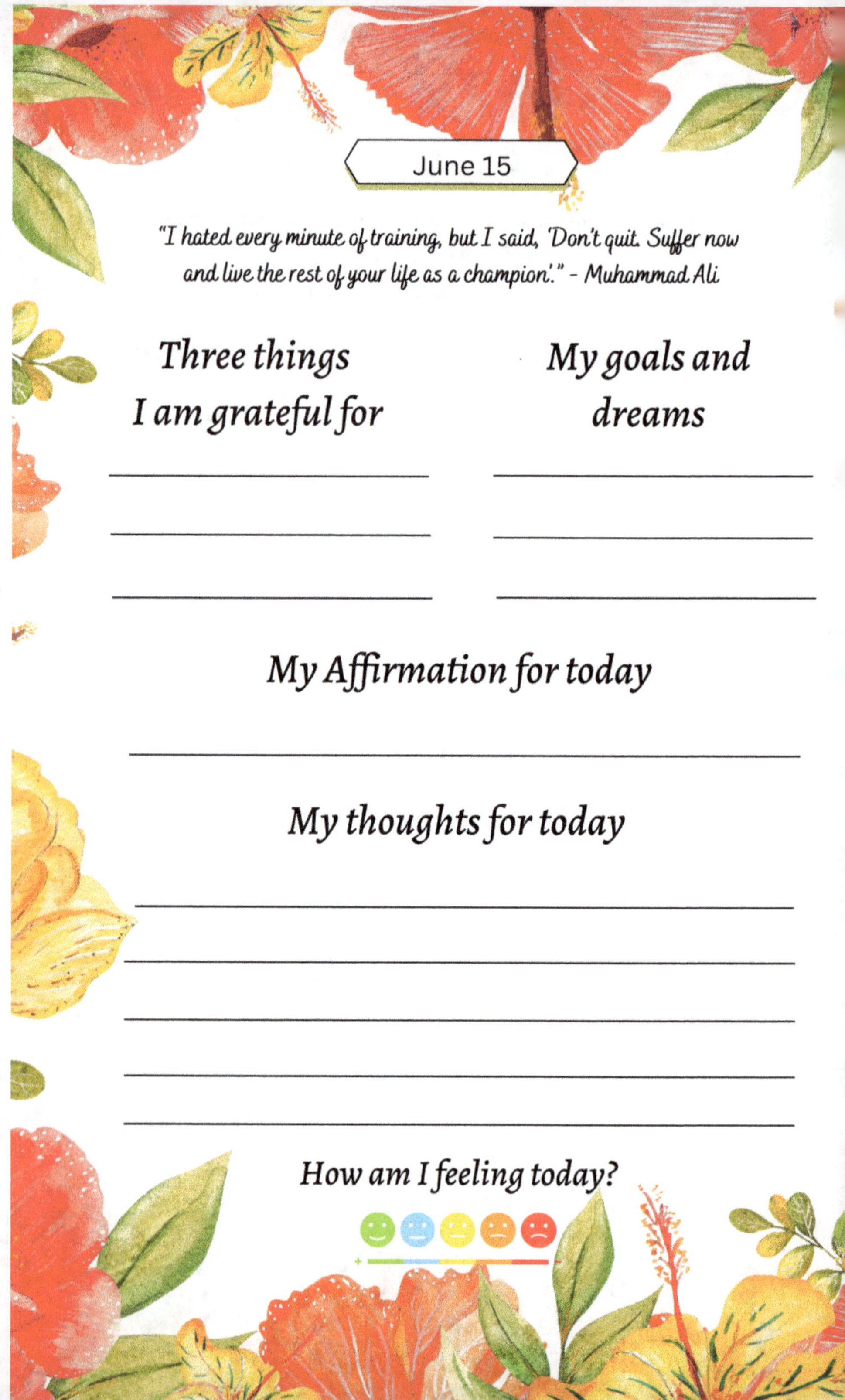

June 15

"I hated every minute of training, but I said, 'Don't quit. Suffer now and live the rest of your life as a champion'." - Muhammad Ali

Three things I am grateful for

My goals and dreams

My Affirmation for today

My thoughts for today

How am I feeling today?

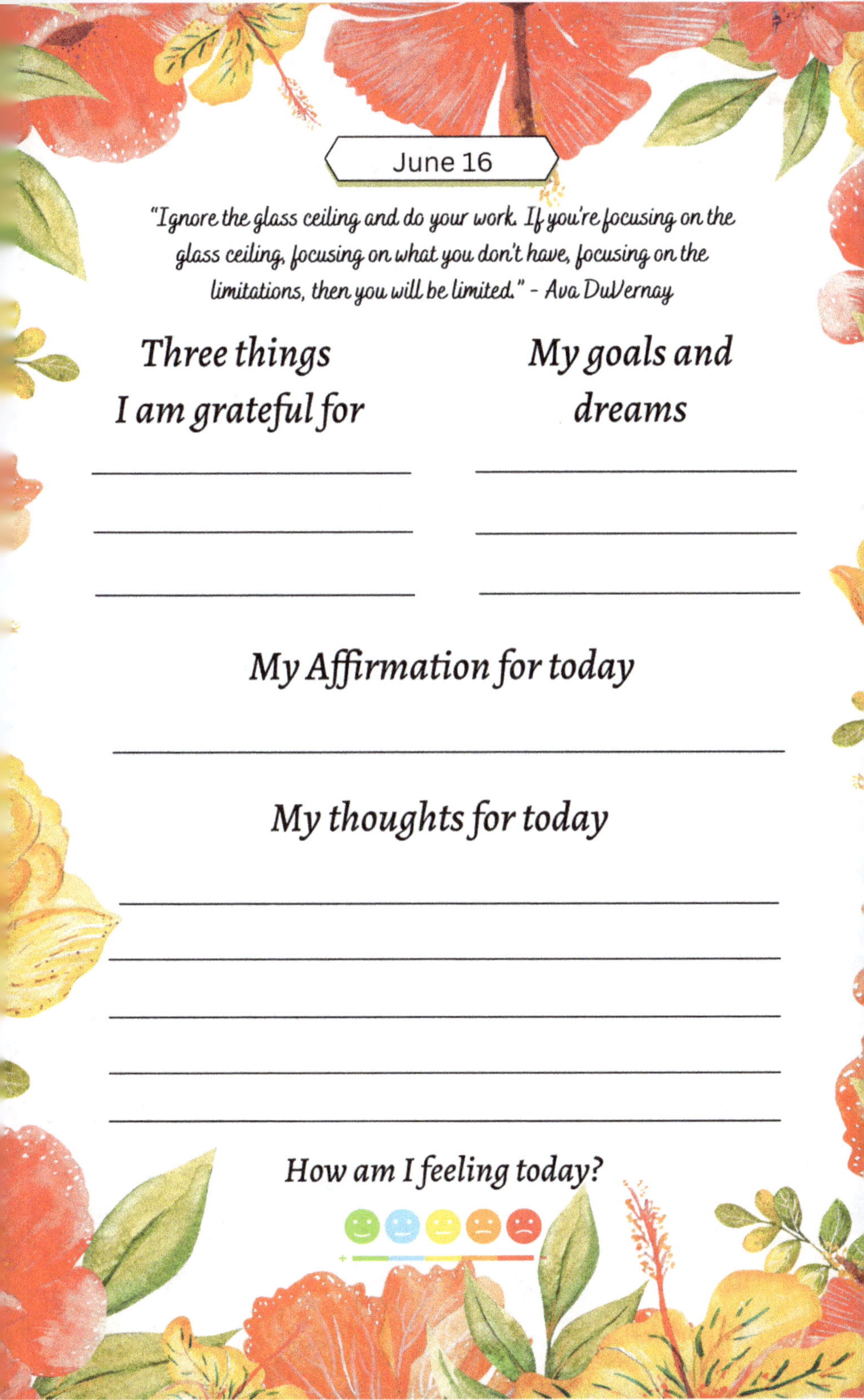

June 16

"Ignore the glass ceiling and do your work. If you're focusing on the glass ceiling, focusing on what you don't have, focusing on the limitations, then you will be limited." - Ava DuVernay

Three things I am grateful for

____

____

____

My goals and dreams

____

____

____

My Affirmation for today

____

My thoughts for today

____

____

____

____

____

How am I feeling today?

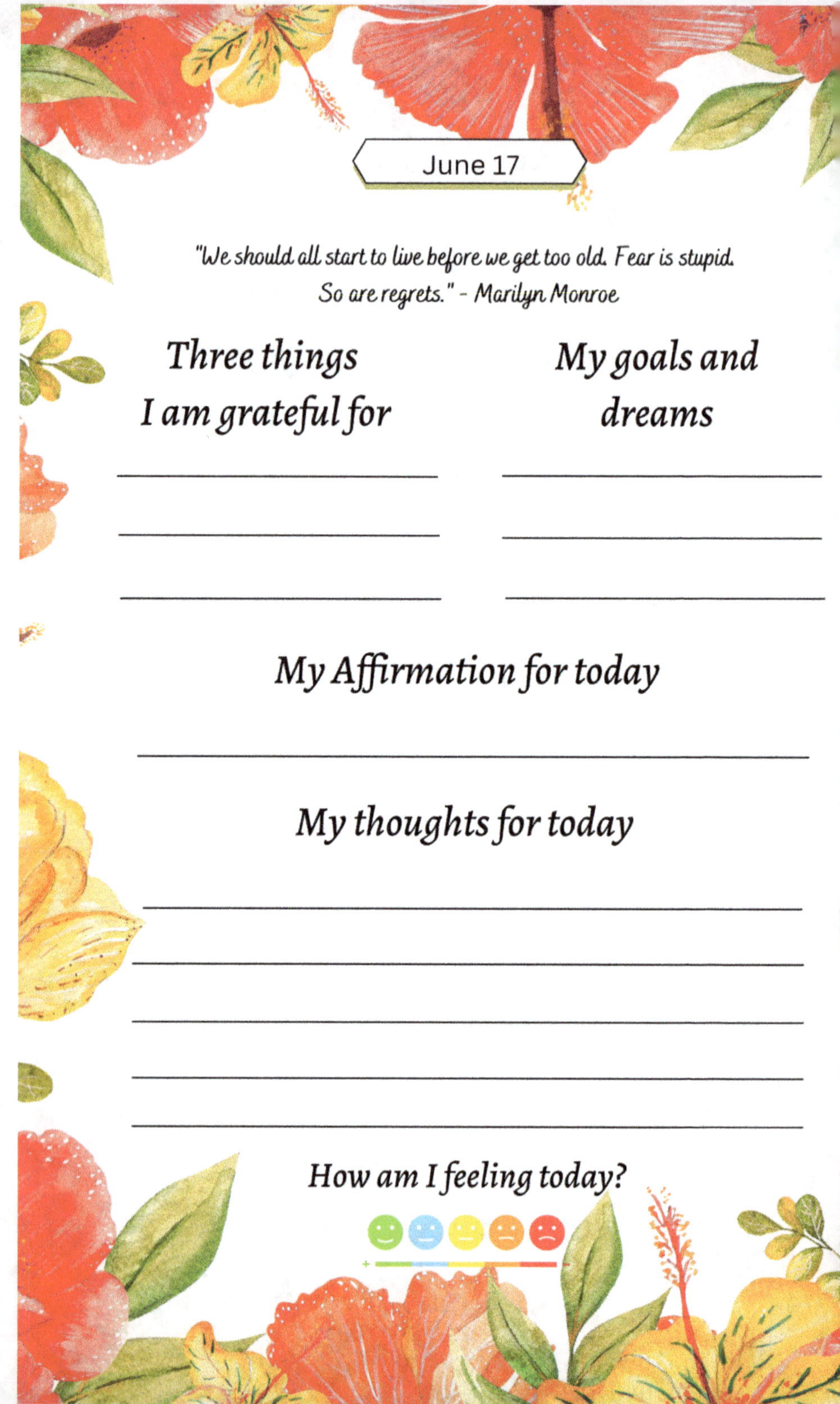

June 17

"We should all start to live before we get too old. Fear is stupid. So are regrets." - Marilyn Monroe

Three things I am grateful for

My goals and dreams

My Affirmation for today

My thoughts for today

How am I feeling today?

June 18

"If people talk behind your back, it's because you're ahead of them."
Zayn Malik

Three things I am grateful for

My goals and dreams

My Affirmation for today

My thoughts for today

How am I feeling today?

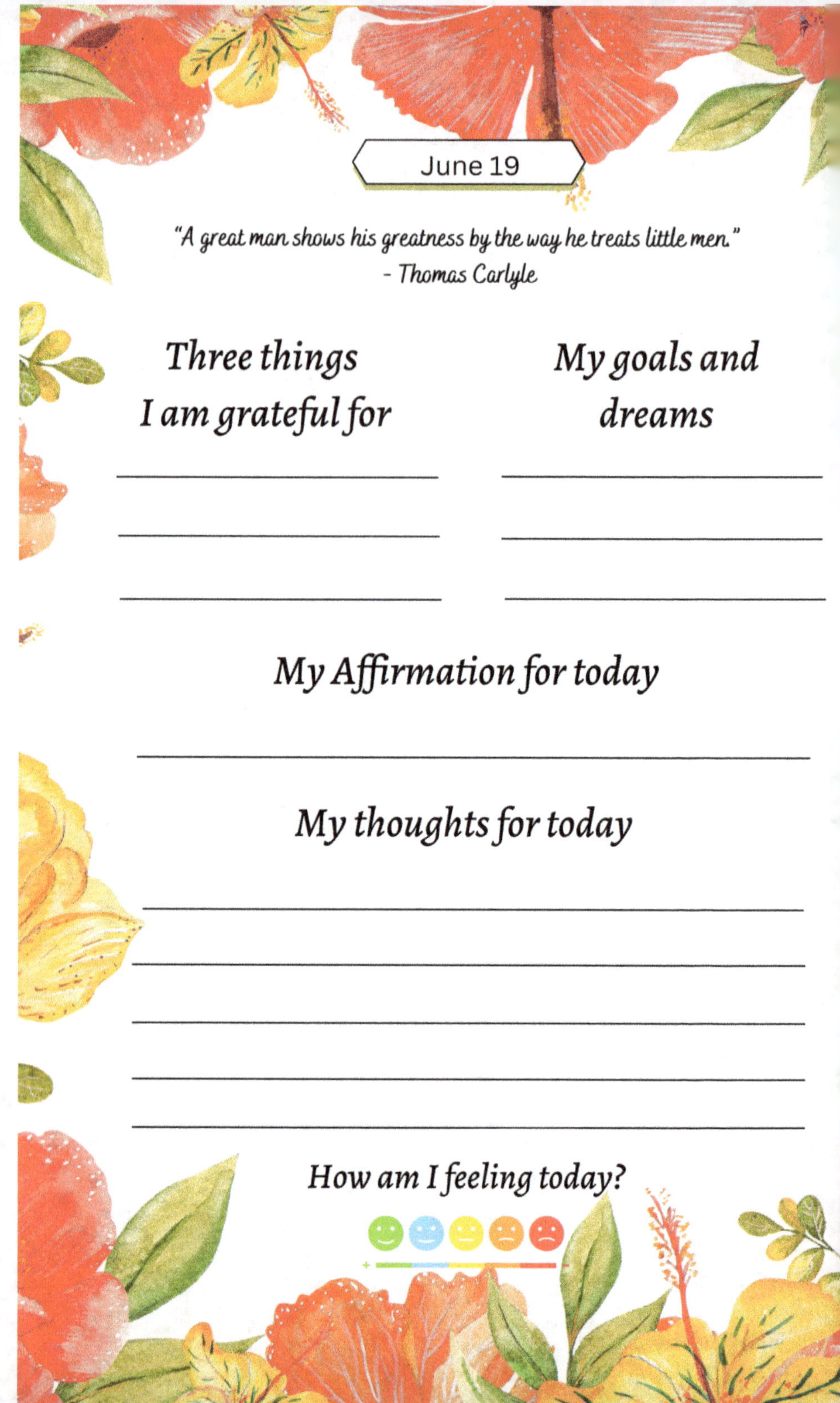

June 19

"A great man shows his greatness by the way he treats little men."
- Thomas Carlyle

Three things I am grateful for

My goals and dreams

My Affirmation for today

My thoughts for today

How am I feeling today?

June 20

"A strong woman knows she has strength enough for the journey, but a woman of strength knows it is in the journey where she will become strong." - Unknown

Three things I am grateful for

My goals and dreams

My Affirmation for today

My thoughts for today

How am I feeling today?

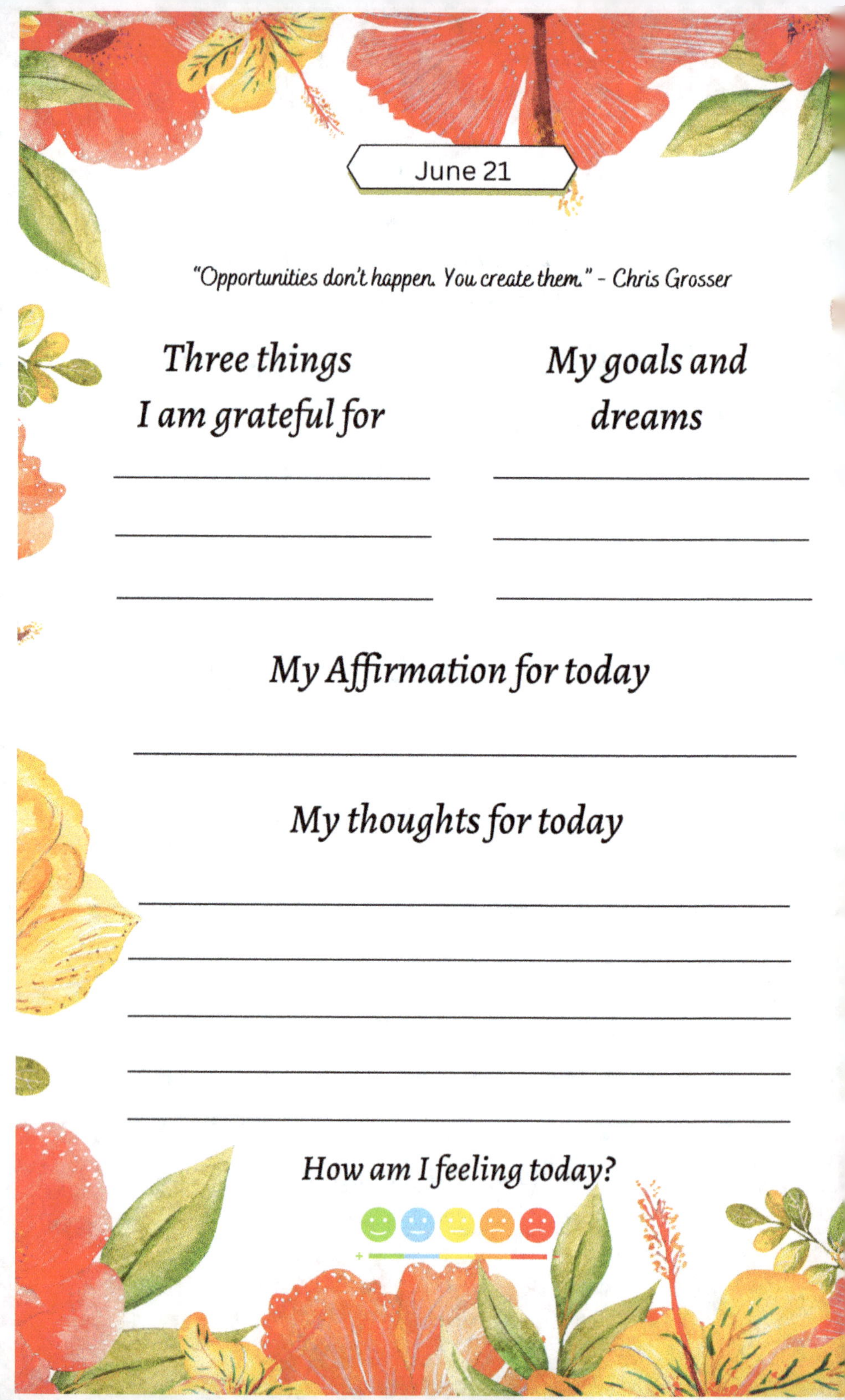

June 21

"Opportunities don't happen. You create them." - Chris Grosser

Three things I am grateful for

____

____

____

My goals and dreams

____

____

____

My Affirmation for today

____

My thoughts for today

____

____

____

____

____

How am I feeling today?

June 22

"I believe in one thing—that only a life lived for others is a life worth living.". - Albert Einstein

Three things I am grateful for

My goals and dreams

My Affirmation for today

My thoughts for today

How am I feeling today?

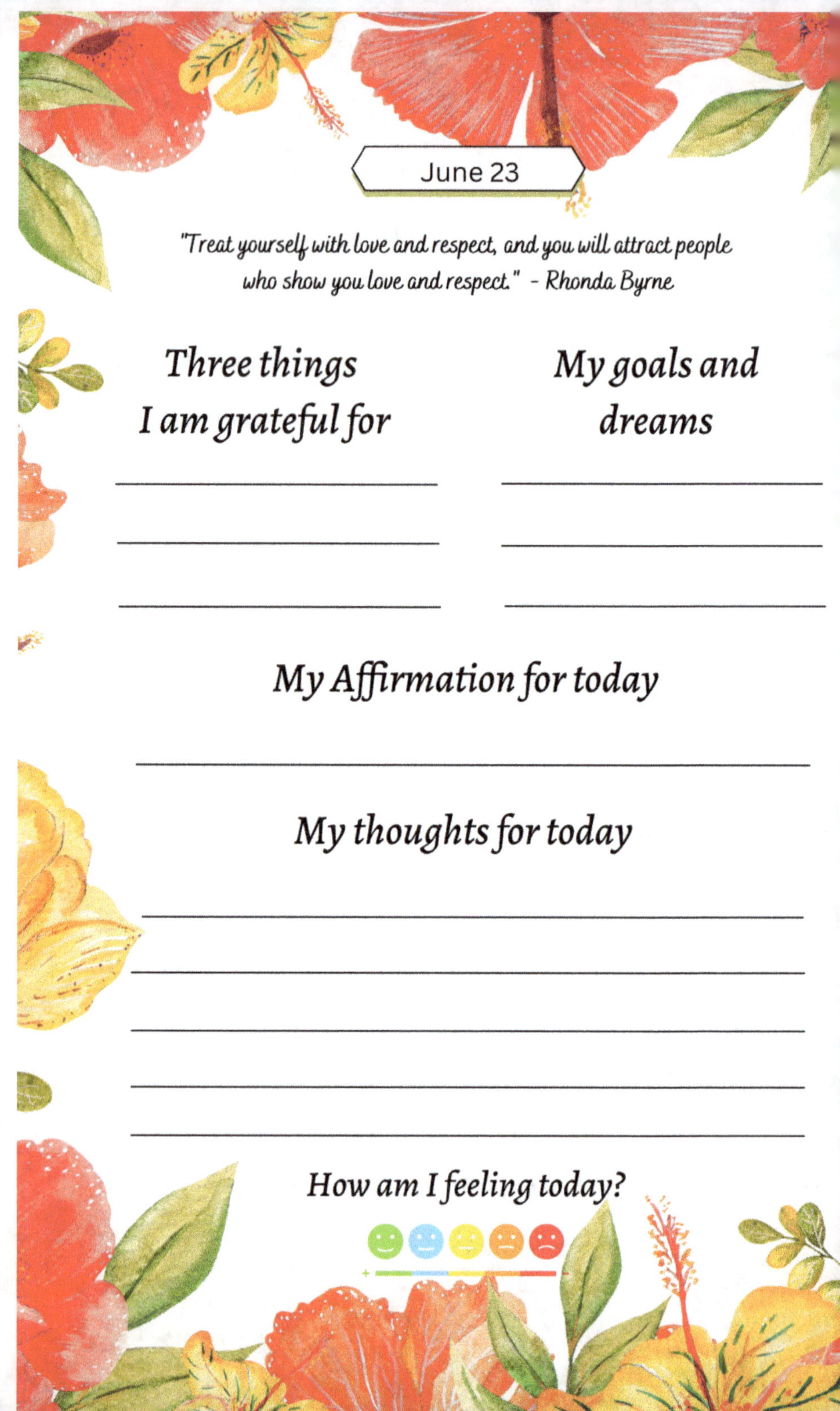

June 23

"Treat yourself with love and respect, and you will attract people who show you love and respect." - Rhonda Byrne

Three things I am grateful for

___

___

___

My goals and dreams

___

___

___

My Affirmation for today

___

My thoughts for today

___

___

___

___

___

How am I feeling today?

June 24

"Success is liking yourself, liking what you do, and liking how you do it."
- Maya Angelou

Three things I am grateful for

My goals and dreams

My Affirmation for today

My thoughts for today

How am I feeling today?

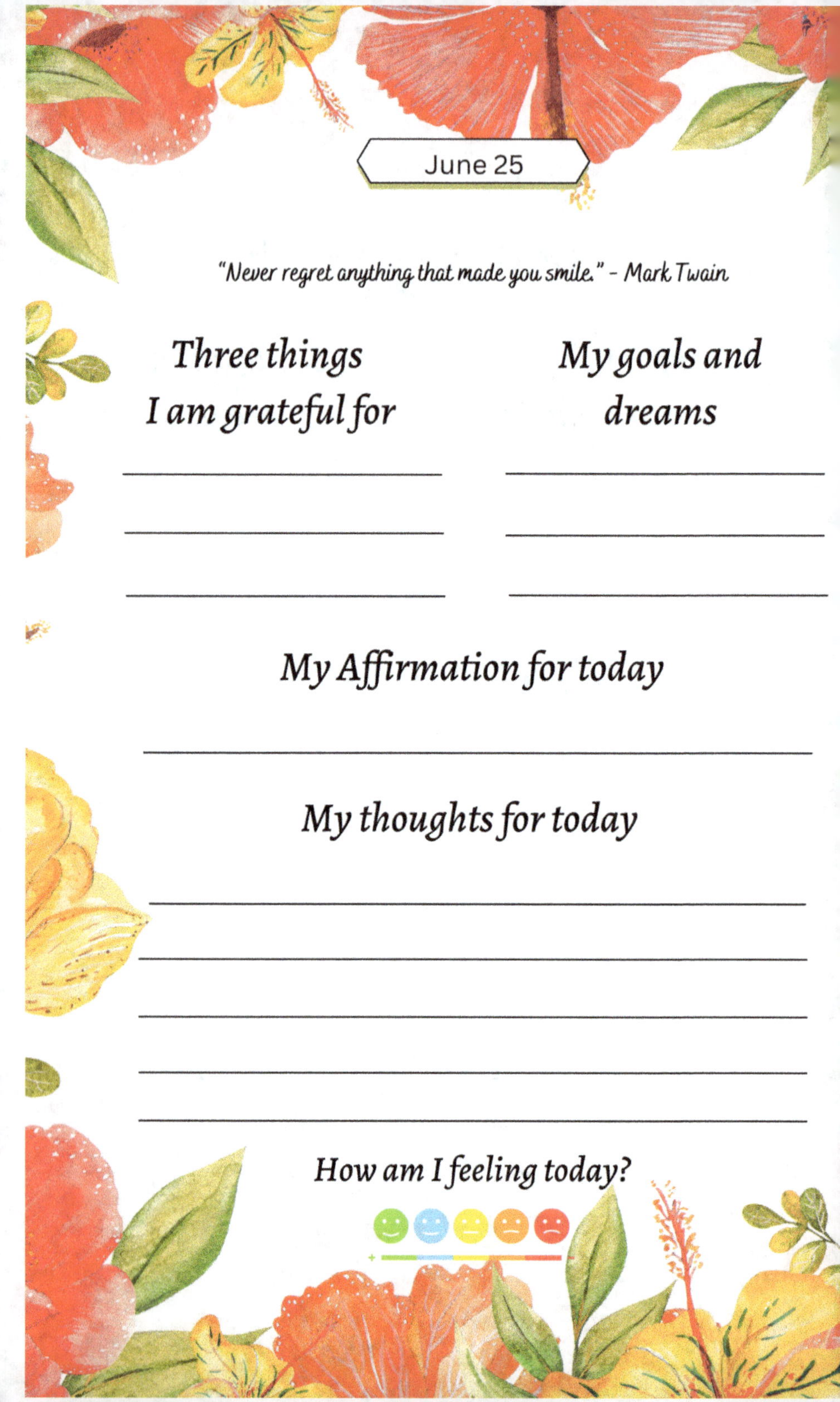

June 25

"Never regret anything that made you smile." - Mark Twain

Three things I am grateful for

My goals and dreams

My Affirmation for today

My thoughts for today

How am I feeling today?

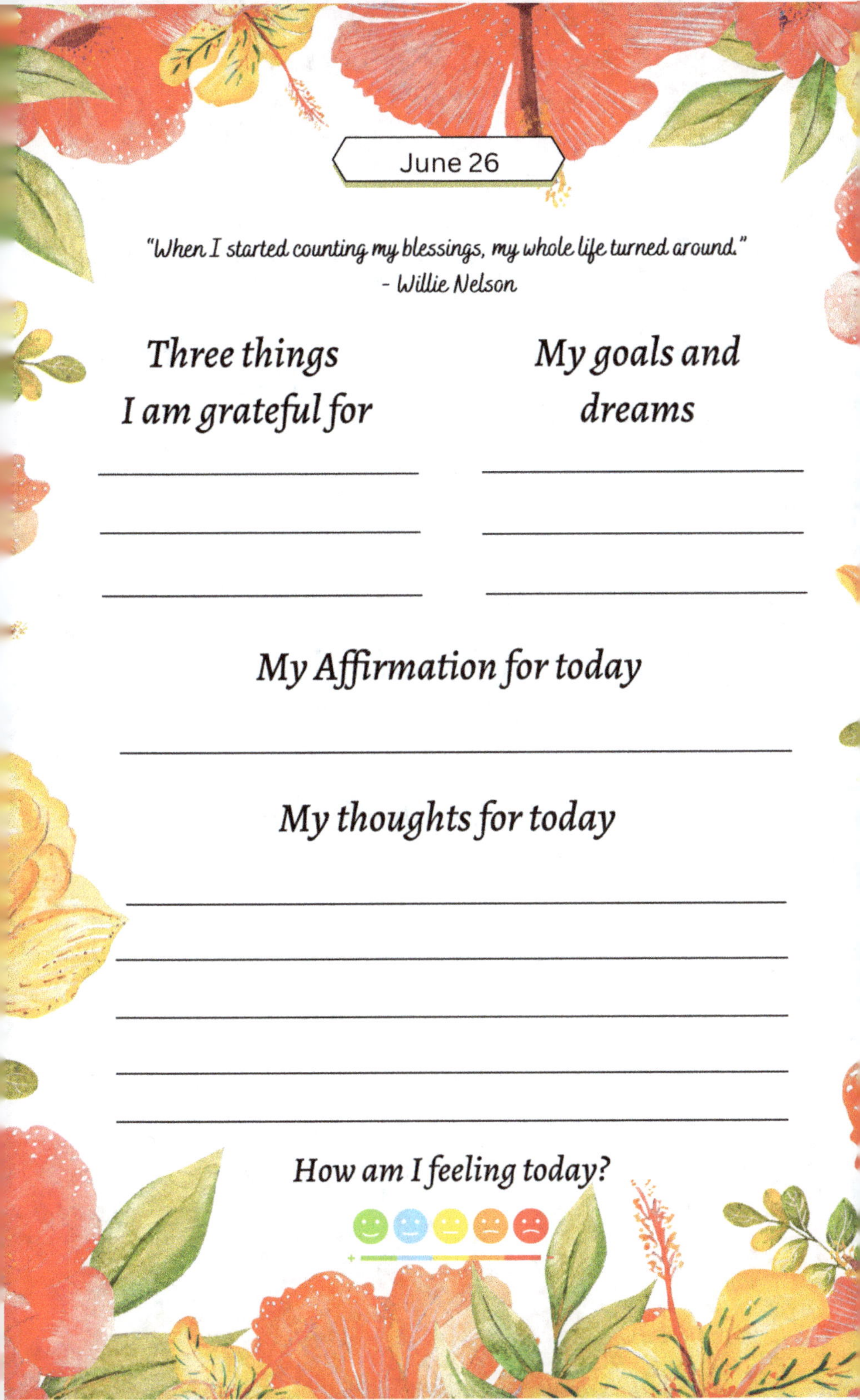

June 26

"When I started counting my blessings, my whole life turned around."
- Willie Nelson

Three things I am grateful for

My goals and dreams

My Affirmation for today

My thoughts for today

How am I feeling today?

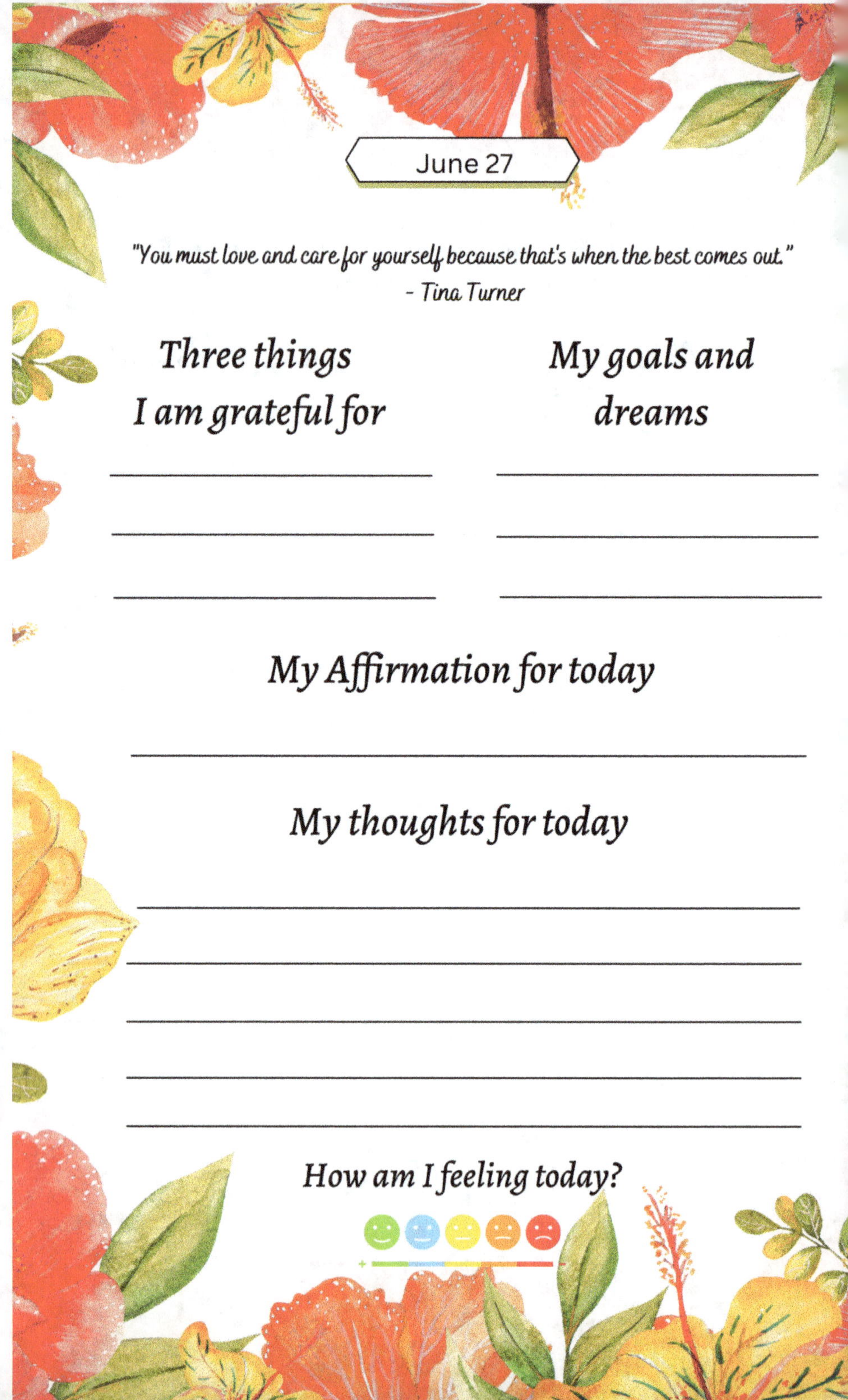

June 27

"You must love and care for yourself because that's when the best comes out."
- Tina Turner

Three things I am grateful for

My goals and dreams

My Affirmation for today

My thoughts for today

How am I feeling today?

June 28

"Never look down on anybody unless you're helping them up"
- Jesse Jackson

Three things I am grateful for

____

____

____

My goals and dreams

____

____

____

My Affirmation for today

____

My thoughts for today

____

____

____

____

____

How am I feeling today?

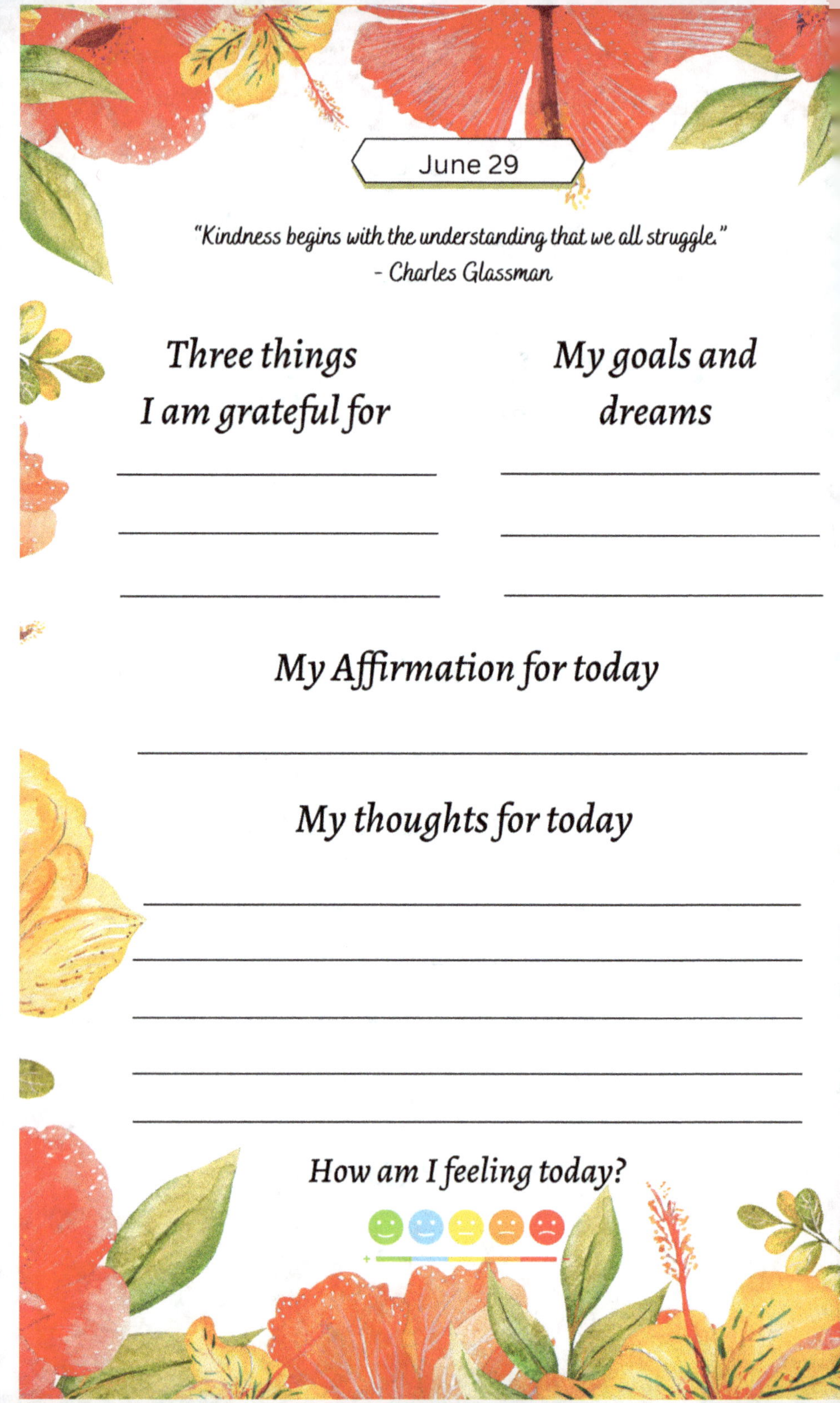

June 29

"Kindness begins with the understanding that we all struggle."
- Charles Glassman

Three things I am grateful for

____

____

____

My goals and dreams

____

____

____

My Affirmation for today

____

My thoughts for today

____

____

____

____

____

How am I feeling today?

June 30

"Kindness is one thing you can't give away. It always comes back."
- George Skolsky

Three things I am grateful for

My goals and dreams

My Affirmation for today

My thoughts for today

How am I feeling today?

JULY 1

"Carry out a random act of kindness, with no expectation of reward, safe in the knowledge that one day someone might do the same for you." - Princess Diana

Three things I am grateful for today

My goals and dreams

My Affirmation for today

My thoughts for today

How am I feeling today?

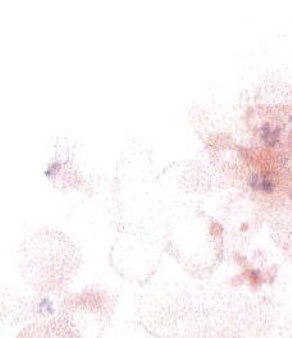

JULY 2

"Kindness is a passport that opens doors and fashions friends. It softens hearts and molds relationships that can last lifetimes."
- Joseph B. Wirthlin

Three things I am grateful for today

My goals and dreams

My Affirmation for today

My thoughts for today

How am I feeling today?

JULY 3

"If you want to fly, give up everything that weighs you down."
- Buddha

Three things I am grateful for today

My goals and dreams

My Affirmation for today

My thoughts for today

How am I feeling today?

JULY 4

"Kind words do not cost much. Yet they accomplish much."
- Blaise Pascal

Three things I am grateful for today

My goals and dreams

My Affirmation for today

My thoughts for today

How am I feeling today?

JULY 5

"What we all have in common is an appreciation of kindness and compassion; all the religions have this. Love. We all lean towards love." - Richard Gere

Three things I am grateful for today

My goals and dreams

My Affirmation for today

My thoughts for today

How am I feeling today?

JULY 6

"Too often we underestimate the power of a touch, a smile, a kind word, a listening ear, an honest compliment, or the smallest act of caring, all of which have the potential to turn a life around." - Leo Buscaglia

Three things I am grateful for today

My goals and dreams

My Affirmation for today

My thoughts for today

How am I feeling today?

JULY 7

"I never lose. Either I win or learn."
- Nelson Mandela

Three things I am grateful for today

My goals and dreams

My Affirmation for today

My thoughts for today

How am I feeling today?

JULY 8

"Girls should never be afraid to be smart."
- Emma Watson

Three things I am grateful for today

My goals and dreams

My Affirmation for today

My thoughts for today

How am I feeling today?

JULY 9

"It always seems impossible until it's done."
- Nelson Mandela

Three things I am grateful for today

My goals and dreams

My Affirmation for today

My thoughts for today

How am I feeling today?

JULY 10

"Courage is resistance to fear, mastery of fear—not absence of fear."
- Mark Twain

Three things I am grateful for today

My goals and dreams

My Affirmation for today

My thoughts for today

How am I feeling today?

JULY 11

"Make your fear of losing your greatest motivator." - Unknown

Three things I am grateful for today

My goals and dreams

My Affirmation for today

My thoughts for today

How am I feeling today?

JULY 12

"Today is your opportunity to build the tomorrow you want." - Ken Poirot

Three things I am grateful for today

My goals and dreams

My Affirmation for today

My thoughts for today

How am I feeling today?

JULY 13

"You don't need to see the whole staircase, just take the first step."
- Martin Luther King Jr.

Three things I am grateful for today

My goals and dreams

My Affirmation for today

My thoughts for today

How am I feeling today?

\+ –

JULY 14

"Plant as many good thoughts as you can in each day."
- Rhonda Byrne

Three things I am grateful for today

My goals and dreams

My Affirmation for today

My thoughts for today

How am I feeling today?

JULY 15

"I didn't get there by wishing for it, but by working for it."
- Estée Lauder

Three things I am grateful for today

My goals and dreams

My Affirmation for today

My thoughts for today

How am I feeling today?

JULY 16

"For attractive lips, speak words of kindness. For lovely eyes, seek out the good in people. For a slim figure, share your food with the hungry. For beautiful hair, let a child run his fingers through it once a day. For poise, walk with the knowledge that you will never walk alone" - Sam Levenson

Three things I am grateful for today

My goals and dreams

My Affirmation for today

My thoughts for today

How am I feeling today?

JULY 17

"She remembered who she was and the game changed."
- Lalah Deliah

Three things I am grateful for today

My goals and dreams

My Affirmation for today

My thoughts for today

How am I feeling today?

JULY 18

"I choose to make the rest of my life the best of my life."
- Louise Hay

Three things I am grateful for today

My goals and dreams

My Affirmation for today

My thoughts for today

How am I feeling today?

JULY 19

"You never know what you can do until you try."
- William Cobbett

Three things I am grateful for today

My goals and dreams

My Affirmation for today

My thoughts for today

How am I feeling today?

JULY 20

"The difference between who you are and who you want to be is what you do."
- Unknown

Three things I am grateful for today

My goals and dreams

My Affirmation for today

My thoughts for today

How am I feeling today?

JULY 21

"Twenty years from now you'll be more disappointed by the things you did not do than the ones you did." - Mark Twain

Three things I am grateful for today

My goals and dreams

My Affirmation for today

My thoughts for today

How am I feeling today?

JULY 22

"Life isn't happening to you; life is responding to you."
- Rhonda Byrne

Three things I am grateful for today

My goals and dreams

My Affirmation for today

My thoughts for today

How am I feeling today?

JULY 23

"I am thankful for all of those who said NO to me. It's because of them I'm doing it myself." - Wayne W. Dyer

Three things I am grateful for today

My goals and dreams

My Affirmation for today

My thoughts for today

How am I feeling today?

JULY 24

"A person who never made a mistake never tried anything new."
- Albert Einstein

Three things I am grateful for today

My goals and dreams

My Affirmation for today

My thoughts for today

How am I feeling today?

JULY 25

"Remember that sometimes not getting what you want is a wonderful stroke of luck." - Dalai Lama XIV

Three things I am grateful for today

My goals and dreams

My Affirmation for today

My thoughts for today

How am I feeling today?

JULY 26

"The most courageous act is still to think for yourself. Aloud." - Coco Chanel

Three things I am grateful for today

My goals and dreams

My Affirmation for today

My thoughts for today

How am I feeling today?

JULY 27

"The world is full of nice people. If you can't find one, be one."
- Nishan Panwar

Three things I am grateful for today

____

____

____

My goals and dreams

____

____

____

My Affirmation for today

____

My thoughts for today

____

____

____

____

____

How am I feeling today?

JULY 28

"If you can't do anything about it then let it go. Don't be a prisoner to things you can't change" - Tony Gaskins

Three things I am grateful for today

My goals and dreams

My Affirmation for today

My thoughts for today

How am I feeling today?

JULY 29

"You can't go back and change the beginning, but you can start where you are and change the ending." - C.S. Lewis

Three things I am grateful for today

___

___

___

My goals and dreams

___

___

___

My Affirmation for today

___

My thoughts for today

___

___

___

___

___

How am I feeling today?

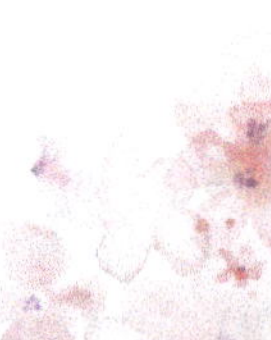

JULY 30

"Yesterday I was clever, so I wanted to change the world. Today I am wise, so I am changing myself." - Rumi

Three things I am grateful for today

My goals and dreams

My Affirmation for today

My thoughts for today

How am I feeling today?

JULY 31

"Practice random kindness and senseless acts of beauty."
- Anne Herbert

Three things I am grateful for today

My goals and dreams

My Affirmation for today

My thoughts for today

How am I feeling today?

\+ –

AUGUST 1

"Don't wait around for other people to be happy for you. Any happiness you get you've got to make yourself" - Alice Walker

Three things I am grateful for today

My goals and dreams

My Affirmation for today

My thoughts for today

How am I feeling today?

AUGUST 2

"A little thought and a little kindness are
often worth more than
a great deal of money." - John Ruskin

Three things I am grateful for today

My goals and dreams

My Affirmation for today

My thoughts for today

How am I feeling today?

\+ –

AUGUST 3

"Joy attracts more joy. Happiness attracts more happiness.
Peace attracts more peace.
GRATITUDE attracts more GRATITUDE.
Kindness attracts more kindness.
Love attracts more love" - Rhonda Byrne

Three things I am grateful for today

My goals and dreams

My Affirmation for today

My thoughts for today

How am I feeling today?

\+ –

AUGUST 4

"And, when you want something, all the universe conspires in helping you to achieve it" - Paulo Coelho, The Alchemist

Three things I am grateful for today

My goals and dreams

My Affirmation for today

My thoughts for today

How am I feeling today?

\+ –

AUGUST 5

"Stop being afraid of what can go wrong and
start being positive about
what can go right." - Unknown

Three things I am grateful for today

My goals and dreams

My Affirmation for today

My thoughts for today

How am I feeling today?

\+ −

AUGUST 6

"Darkness cannot drive out darkness: only light can do that.
Hate cannot drive out hate:
only love can do that." - Martin Luther King Jr.

Three things I am grateful for today

My goals and dreams

My Affirmation for today

My thoughts for today

How am I feeling today?

\+ –

AUGUST 7

"Kindness is always fashionable, and always welcome."
- Amelia Barr

Three things I am grateful for today

My goals and dreams

My Affirmation for today

My thoughts for today

How am I feeling today?

\+ –

AUGUST 8

"Love doesn't make the world go round.
Love is what makes the
ride worthwhile." - Franklin P. Jones

Three things I am grateful for today

My goals and dreams

My Affirmation for today

My thoughts for today

How am I feeling today?

AUGUST 9

"When words are both true and kind,
they can change the world."
- Buddha

Three things I am grateful for today

My goals and dreams

My Affirmation for today

My thoughts for today

How am I feeling today?

AUGUST 10

"It is never too late to be what
you might have been."
- George Eliot

Three things I am grateful for today

My goals and dreams

____

____

____

____

____

____

My Affirmation for today

____

My thoughts for today

____

____

____

____

____

How am I feeling today?

\+ –

AUGUST 11

"If you spend too much time thinking about a thing,
you'll never get it done.
Make at least one definite move
daily toward your goal." - Bruce Lee

Three things I am grateful for today

My goals and dreams

My Affirmation for today

My thoughts for today

How am I feeling today?

+ –

AUGUST 12

"There is some good in this world, and it's worth fighting for."
- J.R.R. Tolkien

Three things I am grateful for today

My goals and dreams

My Affirmation for today

My thoughts for today

How am I feeling today?

AUGUST 13

"What I want young women and girls to know is:
You are powerful and your voice matters.
You're going to walk into many rooms where you
may be the only one who looks like you
or who has had the experiences you've had. So you use that voice
and be strong." - Kamala Harris

Three things I am grateful for today

My goals and dreams

My Affirmation for today

My thoughts for today

How am I feeling today?

\+ −

AUGUST 14

"Oh yes, the past can hurt. But the way I see it, you can either run from it or learn from it." - The Lion King

Three things I am grateful for today

My goals and dreams

My Affirmation for today

My thoughts for today

How am I feeling today?

+ –

AUGUST 15

"If you truly pour your heart into what you believe in, even if it makes you vulnerable, amazing things can and will happen." - Emma Watson

Three things I am grateful for today

My goals and dreams

My Affirmation for today

My thoughts for today

How am I feeling today?

AUGUST 16

"Go and love someone exactly as they are.
And then watch how quickly they transform into the greatest,
truest version of themselves.
When one feels seen and appreciated
in their own essence,
one is instantly empowered" - Wes Angelozzi

Three things I am grateful for today

My goals and dreams

My Affirmation for today

My thoughts for today

How am I feeling today?

\+ –

AUGUST 17

"The most sincere compliment we can pay is attention."
- Walter Anderson

Three things I am grateful for today

My goals and dreams

My Affirmation for today

My thoughts for today

How am I feeling today?

\+ –

AUGUST 18

"Kindness gives birth to kindness."
- Sophocles

Three things I am grateful for today

My goals and dreams

My Affirmation for today

My thoughts for today

How am I feeling today?

\+ –

AUGUST 19

"Sometimes it takes only one act of kindness and
caring to change
a person's life" - Jackie Chan

Three things I am grateful for today

My goals and dreams

My Affirmation for today

My thoughts for today

How am I feeling today?

AUGUST 20

"Life moves pretty fast. If you don't stop and look around
once in a while,
you could miss it" - Ferris Bueller's Day Off

Three things I am grateful for today

My goals and dreams

My Affirmation for today

My thoughts for today

How am I feeling today?

+ –

AUGUST 21

"Once I learned to like me more than others did, then I didn't have to worry about being the funniest or the most popular or the prettiest. I was the best me and I only ever tried to be that" - Issa Rae

Three things I am grateful for today

My goals and dreams

My Affirmation for today

My thoughts for today

How am I feeling today?

\+ −

AUGUST 22

"He who is not courageous enough to take risks
will accomplish
nothing in life." - Muhammad Ali

Three things I am grateful for today

My goals and dreams

My Affirmation for today

My thoughts for today

How am I feeling today?

AUGUST 23

"I don't want other people to decide who I am. I want to decide that for myself" - Emma Watson

Three things I am grateful for today

My goals and dreams

My Affirmation for today

My thoughts for today

How am I feeling today?

\+ −

AUGUST 24

"A woman knows by intuition, or instinct, what is best for herself."
- Marilyn Monroe

Three things I am grateful for today

My goals and dreams

My Affirmation for today

My thoughts for today

How am I feeling today?

\+ –

AUGUST 25

"Always be a little kinder than necessary."
- James M. Barrie

Three things I am grateful for today

My goals and dreams

My Affirmation for today

My thoughts for today

How am I feeling today?

\+ −

AUGUST 26

"Spend a little more time trying to do
something with yourself
and a little less time trying to
impress people." - The Breakfast Club

Three things I am grateful for today

My goals and dreams

My Affirmation for today

My thoughts for today

How am I feeling today?

\+ –

AUGUST 27

"The problem is not the problem. The problem is your attitude about the problem" - Pirates of the Caribbean

Three things I am grateful for today

My goals and dreams

My Affirmation for today

My thoughts for today

How am I feeling today?

\+ −

AUGUST 28

"A kind word is like a spring day."
- Russian proverb

Three things I am grateful for today

My goals and dreams

My Affirmation for today

My thoughts for today

How am I feeling today?

AUGUST 29

"Remember you're the one who can fill the world with sunshine."
- Snow White and the Seven Dwarfs

Three things I am grateful for today

My goals and dreams

My Affirmation for today

My thoughts for today

How am I feeling today?

AUGUST 30

"It takes a great deal of bravery to stand up to our enemies but just as much to stand up to our friends." - J.K. Rowling

Three things I am grateful for today

My goals and dreams

My Affirmation for today

My thoughts for today

How am I feeling today?

+ –

AUGUST 31

"Kindness is more important than wisdom, and the recognition of this is the beginning of wisdom" - Theodore Isaac Rubin

Three things I am grateful for today

My goals and dreams

My Affirmation for today

My thoughts for today

How am I feeling today?

\+ –

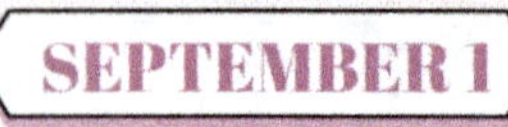

SEPTEMBER 1

"Do something today that your future self will thank you for."

- Unknown

Three things I am grateful for today

My goals and dreams

My Affirmation for today

My thoughts for today

How am I feeling today?

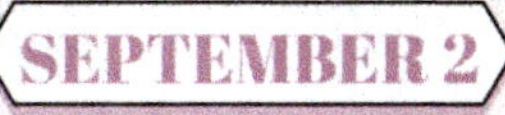

SEPTEMBER 2

"Gratitude is the inward feeling of kindness received.
Thankfulness is the natural impulse to express that feeling.
Thanksgiving is the following of that impulse." - Henry van Dyke

Three things I am grateful for today

My goals and dreams

My Affirmation for today

My thoughts for today

How am I feeling today?

+ −

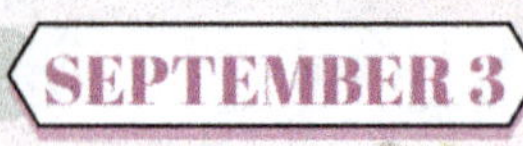

SEPTEMBER 3

"You yourself, as much as anybody in the entire universe, deserve your love and affection." - Buddha

Three things I am grateful for today

My goals and dreams

My Affirmation for today

My thoughts for today

How am I feeling today?

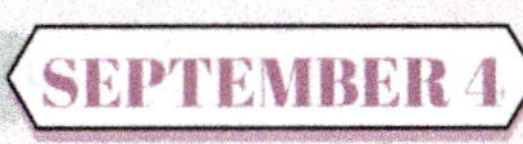

SEPTEMBER 4

"Try not to become a man of success, but rather become a man of value."

- Albert Einstein

Three things I am grateful for today

My goals and dreams

My Affirmation for today

My thoughts for today

How am I feeling today?

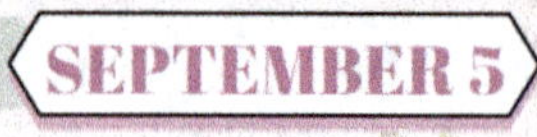

SEPTEMBER 5

"The most alluring thing a woman can have is confidence."
- Beyoncé Knowles

Three things I am grateful for today

My goals and dreams

My Affirmation for today

My thoughts for today

How am I feeling today?

\+ –

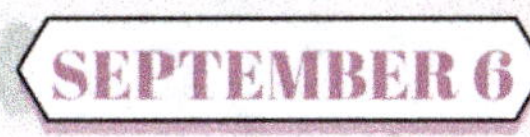

SEPTEMBER 6

"Unexpected kindness is the most powerful, least costly, and most underrated agent of human change." - Bob Kerrey

Three things I am grateful for today

My goals and dreams

My Affirmation for today

My thoughts for today

How am I feeling today?

\+ –

"Confidence is the most beautiful thing you can possess."

- Sabrina Carpenter

Three things I am grateful for today

My goals and dreams

My Affirmation for today

My thoughts for today

How am I feeling today?

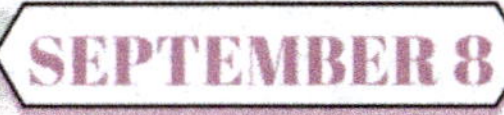

SEPTEMBER 8

"A winner is a dreamer who never gives up."

- Nelson Mandela

Three things I am grateful for today

My goals and dreams

My Affirmation for today

My thoughts for today

How am I feeling today?

+ –

SEPTEMBER 9

"One of the best things that ever happened to me is that I'm a woman. That is the way all females should feel." - Marilyn Monroe

Three things I am grateful for today

My goals and dreams

My Affirmation for today

My thoughts for today

How am I feeling today?

SEPTEMBER 10

"Never let success get to your head; never let failures get to your heart."

- Ziad K. Abdelnour

Three things I am grateful for today

My goals and dreams

My Affirmation for today

My thoughts for today

How am I feeling today?

\+ −

SEPTEMBER 11

"Kindness can become its own motive.
We are made kind by being kind."
- Eric Hoffer

Three things I am grateful for today

My goals and dreams

My Affirmation for today

My thoughts for today

How am I feeling today?

\+ –

SEPTEMBER 12

"Because that's what kindness is. It's not doing something for someone else because they can't, but because you can." - Andrew Iskander

Three things I am grateful for today

My goals and dreams

My Affirmation for today

My thoughts for today

How am I feeling today?

\+ –

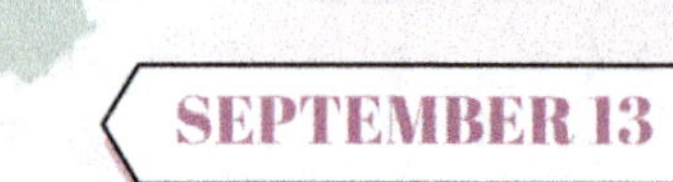

SEPTEMBER 13

"What is life without a little risk?" - J.K. Rowling

Three things I am grateful for today

My goals and dreams

My Affirmation for today

My thoughts for today

How am I feeling today?

+ −

SEPTEMBER 14

"I fear not the man who has practiced 10,000 kicks once,
but I fear the man who has practiced one kick 10,000 times"
- Bruce Lee

Three things I am grateful for today

My goals and dreams

My Affirmation for today

My thoughts for today

How am I feeling today?

+ –

SEPTEMBER 15

"No one can make you feel inferior without your consent." - Eleanor Roosevelt

Three things I am grateful for today

My goals and dreams

My Affirmation for today

My thoughts for today

How am I feeling today?

+ –

SEPTEMBER 16

"That is what compassion does. It challenges our assumptions, our sense of self-limitation, worthlessness, of not having a place in the world, our feelings of loneliness and estrangement. These are narrow, constrictive states of mind. As we develop compassion, our hearts open."- Sharon Salzberg

Three things I am grateful for today

My goals and dreams

My Affirmation for today

My thoughts for today

How am I feeling today?

+ –

SEPTEMBER 17

*"You cannot swim for new horizons
until you have the courage to
lose sight of the shore." - William Faulkner*

Three things I am grateful for today

My goals and dreams

My Affirmation for today

My thoughts for today

How am I feeling today?

\+ −

SEPTEMBER 18

"To love oneself is the beginning of a lifelong romance."

- Oscar Wilde

Three things I am grateful for today

My goals and dreams

My Affirmation for today

My thoughts for today

How am I feeling today?

\+ –

SEPTEMBER 19

"Life shrinks or expands in proportion to one's courage."

- Anaïs Nin

Three things I am grateful for today

My goals and dreams

My Affirmation for today

My thoughts for today

How am I feeling today?

\+ −

SEPTEMBER 20

"Only do what your heart tells you."

- Princess Diana

Three things I am grateful for today

My goals and dreams

My Affirmation for today

My thoughts for today

How am I feeling today?

\+ –

SEPTEMBER 21

"Have confidence that if you have done a little thing well, you can do a bigger thing well too." - David Storey

Three things I am grateful for today

My goals and dreams

My Affirmation for today

My thoughts for today

How am I feeling today?

\+ –

SEPTEMBER 22

"A kind gesture can reach a wound that only compassion can heal" - Steve Maraboli

Three things I am grateful for today

My goals and dreams

My Affirmation for today

My thoughts for today

How am I feeling today?

\+ −

SEPTEMBER 23

"If it's a good idea, go ahead and do it. It's much easier to apologize than it is to get permission." - Grace Hopper

Three things I am grateful for today

My goals and dreams

My Affirmation for today

My thoughts for today

How am I feeling today?

\+ –

SEPTEMBER 24

"I attribute my success to this: I never gave or took an excuse."

- Florence Nightingale

Three things I am grateful for today

My goals and dreams

My Affirmation for today

My thoughts for today

How am I feeling today?

\+ –

SEPTEMBER 25

"The words of kindness are more healing to a drooping heart than balm or honey." - Sarah Fielding

Three things I am grateful for today

My goals and dreams

My Affirmation for today

My thoughts for today

How am I feeling today?

\+ –

"Courage is grace under pressure."

- Ernest Hemingway

Three things I am grateful for today

My goals and dreams

My Affirmation for today

My thoughts for today

How am I feeling today?

SEPTEMBER 27

"Never regret a day in your life. Good days
bring you happiness
and bad days give you experience." - Unknown

Three things I am grateful for today

My goals and dreams

My Affirmation for today

My thoughts for today

How am I feeling today?

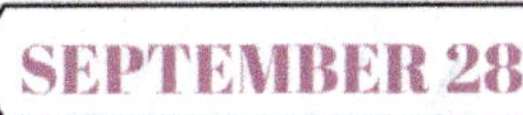

SEPTEMBER 28

"A surplus of effort could overcome a deficit of confidence."

- Sonia Sotomayer

Three things I am grateful for today

My goals and dreams

My Affirmation for today

My thoughts for today

How am I feeling today?

"A problem is a chance for you to do your best."

- Duke Ellington

Three things I am grateful for today

My goals and dreams

My Affirmation for today

My thoughts for today

How am I feeling today?

SEPTEMBER 30

"You cannot do kindness too soon,
for you never know how soon it will be too late."
- Ralph Waldo Emerson

Three things I am grateful for today

My goals and dreams

My Affirmation for today

My thoughts for today

How am I feeling today?

\+ –

OCTOBER 1

"You'll have bad times, but it'll always wake you up to the good stuff you weren't paying attention to." - Good Will Hunting

Three things I am grateful for today

My goals and dreams

My Affirmation for today

My thoughts for today

How am I feeling today?

OCTOBER 2

"If your actions create a legacy that inspires others
to dream more,
learn more, do more and become more,
then, you are an excellent leader." - Dolly Parton

Three things I am grateful for today

My goals and dreams

My Affirmation for today

My thoughts for today

How am I feeling today?

OCTOBER 3

"On my own I will just create and if it works, it works. And if it doesn't, I'll just create something else. I don't have any limitations on what I think I could do or be."

- Oprah Winfrey

Three things I am grateful for today

My goals and dreams

My Affirmation for today

My thoughts for today

How am I feeling today?

\+ –

OCTOBER 4

"Doubt kills more dreams than failure ever will." - Suzy Kassem

Three things I am grateful for today

My goals and dreams

My Affirmation for today

My thoughts for today

How am I feeling today?

OCTOBER 5

"You have to find what sparks a light in you so that you in your own way can illuminate the world." - Oprah Winfrey

Three things I am grateful for today

My goals and dreams

My Affirmation for today

My thoughts for today

How am I feeling today?

OCTOBER 6

"What you are thinking now is creating your future life" - Rhonda Byrne

Three things I am grateful for today

My goals and dreams

My Affirmation for today

My thoughts for today

How am I feeling today?

OCTOBER 7

"Start each day with a positive thought and a grateful heart" - Roy T. Bennett

Three things I am grateful for today

My goals and dreams

My Affirmation for today

My thoughts for today

How am I feeling today?

+ –

"I'd rather regret the risks that didn't work out than the chances I didn't take at all." - Simone Biles

Three things I am grateful for today

My goals and dreams

My Affirmation for today

My thoughts for today

How am I feeling today?

OCTOBER 9

"Done is better than perfect." - Sheryl Sandberg

Three things I am grateful for today

My goals and dreams

My Affirmation for today

My thoughts for today

How am I feeling today?

OCTOBER 10

"If your dreams don't scare you, they are too small"
- Richard Branson

Three things I am grateful for today

My goals and dreams

My Affirmation for today

My thoughts for today

How am I feeling today?

OCTOBER 11

"Kindness is the golden chain by which society is bound together."
- Johann Wolfgang von Goethe.

Three things I am grateful for today

My goals and dreams

My Affirmation for today

My thoughts for today

How am I feeling today?

OCTOBER 12

"Wherever there is a human being, there is an opportunity for kindness" - Lucius Annaeus Seneca

Three things I am grateful for today

My goals and dreams

My Affirmation for today

My thoughts for today

How am I feeling today?

OCTOBER 13

"The world is changed by your example, not by your opinion."
- Paulo Coelho

Three things I am grateful for today

My goals and dreams

My Affirmation for today

My thoughts for today

How am I feeling today?

OCTOBER 14

"If you don't build your dream, someone else will hire you to help them build theirs." - Dhirubhai Ambani

Three things I am grateful for today

My goals and dreams

My Affirmation for today

My thoughts for today

How am I feeling today?

OCTOBER 15

"I'm not in this world to live up to your expectations,
and you're not in this world
to live up to mine" - Bruce Lee

Three things I am grateful for today

My goals and dreams

My Affirmation for today

My thoughts for today

How am I feeling today?

"When you love yourself, people can kind of pick up on that: they can see confidence, they can see self-esteem, and naturally, people gravitate towards you." - Lilly Singh

Three things I am grateful for today

My goals and dreams

My Affirmation for today

My thoughts for today

How am I feeling today?

OCTOBER 17

"What's right is what's left if you do everything else wrong."
- Robin Williams

Three things I am grateful for today

My goals and dreams

My Affirmation for today

My thoughts for today

How am I feeling today?

OCTOBER 18

"Dream beautiful dreams, and then work to make those dreams come true."
- Spencer W. Kimball

Three things I am grateful for today

My goals and dreams

My Affirmation for today

My thoughts for today

How am I feeling today?

+ –

"Women are the real architects of society."
- Cher

Three things I am grateful for today

My goals and dreams

My Affirmation for today

My thoughts for today

How am I feeling today?

OCTOBER 20

"Be the change you want to see in the world."
- Mahatma Gandhi

Three things I am grateful for today

My goals and dreams

My Affirmation for today

My thoughts for today

How am I feeling today?

"Believe you can and you will." - Unknown

Three things I am grateful for today

My goals and dreams

My Affirmation for today

My thoughts for today

How am I feeling today?

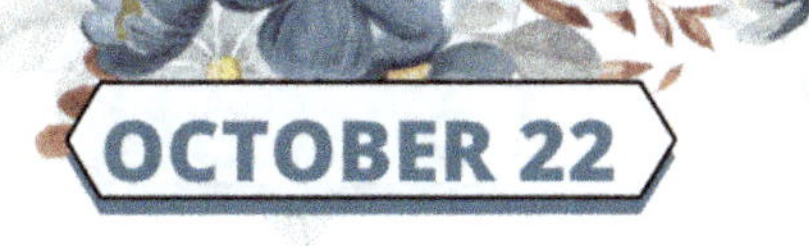

"To be yourself in a world that is constantly trying to make you something else is the greatest accomplishment."

- Ralph Waldo Emerson

Three things I am grateful for today

My goals and dreams

My Affirmation for today

My thoughts for today

How am I feeling today?

OCTOBER 23

"Feeling beautiful has nothing to do with what you look like, I promise."
- Emma Watson

Three things I am grateful for today

My goals and dreams

My Affirmation for today

My thoughts for today

How am I feeling today?

OCTOBER 24

"You can't have a million dollar dream on a minimum wage work ethic."
- Unknown

Three things I am grateful for today

My goals and dreams

My Affirmation for today

My thoughts for today

How am I feeling today?

"As soon as you trust yourself, you will know how to live."

- Johann Wolfgang von Goethe

Three things I am grateful for today

My goals and dreams

My Affirmation for today

My thoughts for today

How am I feeling today?

OCTOBER 26

"You must do the kind of things you think you cannot do."
- Eleanor Roosevelt

Three things I am grateful for today

My goals and dreams

My Affirmation for today

My thoughts for today

How am I feeling today?

"Gratitude is when memory is stored in the heart and not in the mind."
- Lionel Hampton

Three things I am grateful for today

My goals and dreams

My Affirmation for today

My thoughts for today

How am I feeling today?

"Always remember: You are braver than you believe,
stronger than you seem,
and smarter than you think."
- Christopher Robin

Three things I am grateful for today

My goals and dreams

My Affirmation for today

My thoughts for today

How am I feeling today?

OCTOBER 29

"I learned that courage was not the absence of fear but the triumph over it. The brave man is not he who does not feel afraid but he who conquers that fear."
- Nelson Mandela

Three things I am grateful for today

My goals and dreams

My Affirmation for today

My thoughts for today

How am I feeling today?

OCTOBER 30

"If you could get up the courage to begin, you have the courage to succeed."
- David Viscott

Three things I am grateful for today

My goals and dreams

My Affirmation for today

My thoughts for today

How am I feeling today?

OCTOBER 31

"It's not what you do once in a while, it's what you do day in and day out that makes the difference." - Jenny Craig

Three things I am grateful for today

My goals and dreams

My Affirmation for today

My thoughts for today

How am I feeling today?

NOVEMBER 1

"Champions keep playing until they get it right" - Billie Jean King

Three things I am grateful for today

My goals and dreams

My Affirmation for today

My thoughts for today

How am I feeling today?

NOVEMBER 2

"Kindness is the only service that will stand the storm of life and not wash out.
It will wear well and will be remembered long after the prism of politeness or the complexion of courtesy has faded away"- Abraham Lincoln

Three things I am grateful for today

My goals and dreams

My Affirmation for today

My thoughts for today

How am I feeling today?

NOVEMBER 3

*"Scared is what you're feeling.
Brave is what you're doing."*
- Emma Donoghue

Three things I am grateful for today

____

____

____

My goals and dreams

____

____

____

My Affirmation for today

____

My thoughts for today

____

____

____

____

____

How am I feeling today?

"Bravery is being the only one
who knows
you're afraid" - Franklin P. Jones

Three things I am grateful for today

My goals and dreams

My Affirmation for today

My thoughts for today

How am I feeling today?

NOVEMBER 5

"Strong women don't have 'attitudes',
we have standards."
- Marilyn Monroe

Three things I am grateful for today

My goals and dreams

My Affirmation for today

My thoughts for today

How am I feeling today?

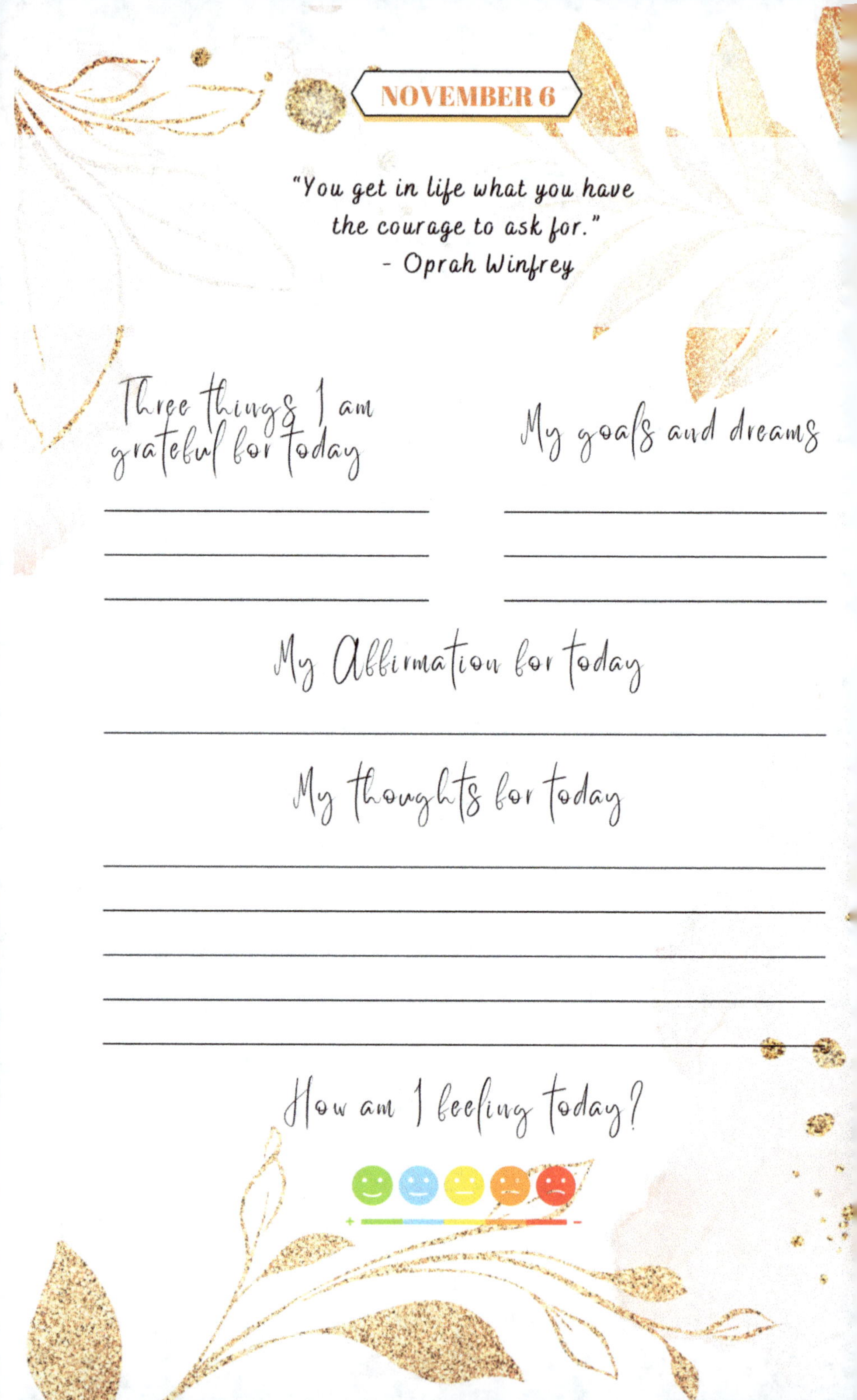

NOVEMBER 6

"You get in life what you have the courage to ask for."
- Oprah Winfrey

Three things I am grateful for today

My goals and dreams

My Affirmation for today

My thoughts for today

How am I feeling today?

+ −

"The greatest weapon against stress is
the ability to choose
one thought over another." - William James

Three things I am grateful for today

My goals and dreams

My Affirmation for today

My thoughts for today

How am I feeling today?

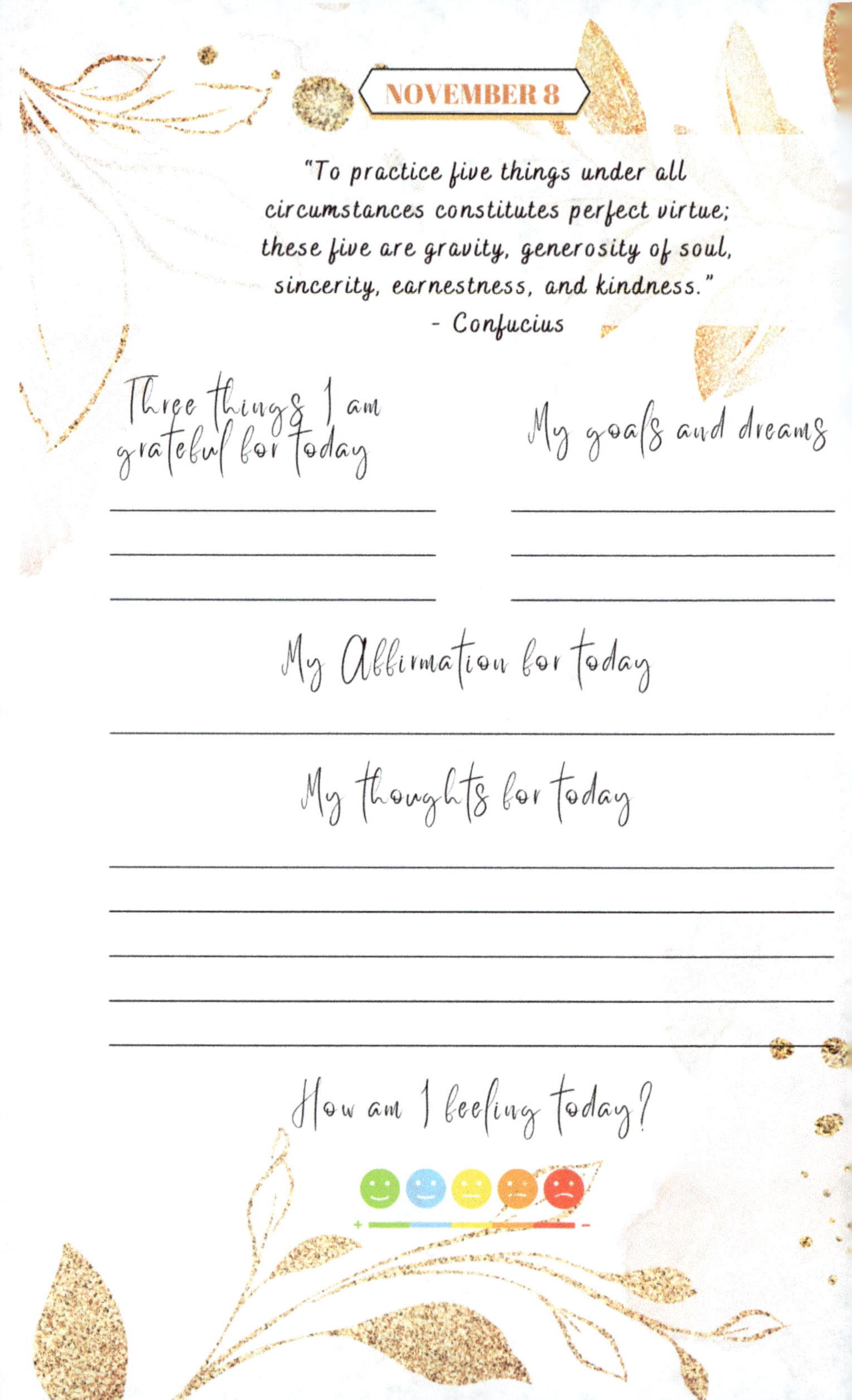

NOVEMBER 8

"To practice five things under all circumstances constitutes perfect virtue; these five are gravity, generosity of soul, sincerity, earnestness, and kindness."
- Confucius

Three things I am grateful for today

My goals and dreams

My Affirmation for today

My thoughts for today

How am I feeling today?

NOVEMBER 9

"Falling down is how we grow.
Staying down is how we die."
- Brian Vaszily

Three things I am grateful for today

My goals and dreams

My Affirmation for today

My thoughts for today

How am I feeling today?

"Get more confidence by doing things that excite and frighten you." - Jessica Williams

Three things I am grateful for today

____

____

____

My goals and dreams

____

____

____

My Affirmation for today

____

My thoughts for today

____

____

____

____

____

How am I feeling today?

"I am learning every day to allow the
space between where I am and where
I want to be to inspire me
and not terrify me." - Tracee Ellis Ross

Three things I am grateful for today

My goals and dreams

My Affirmation for today

My thoughts for today

How am I feeling today?

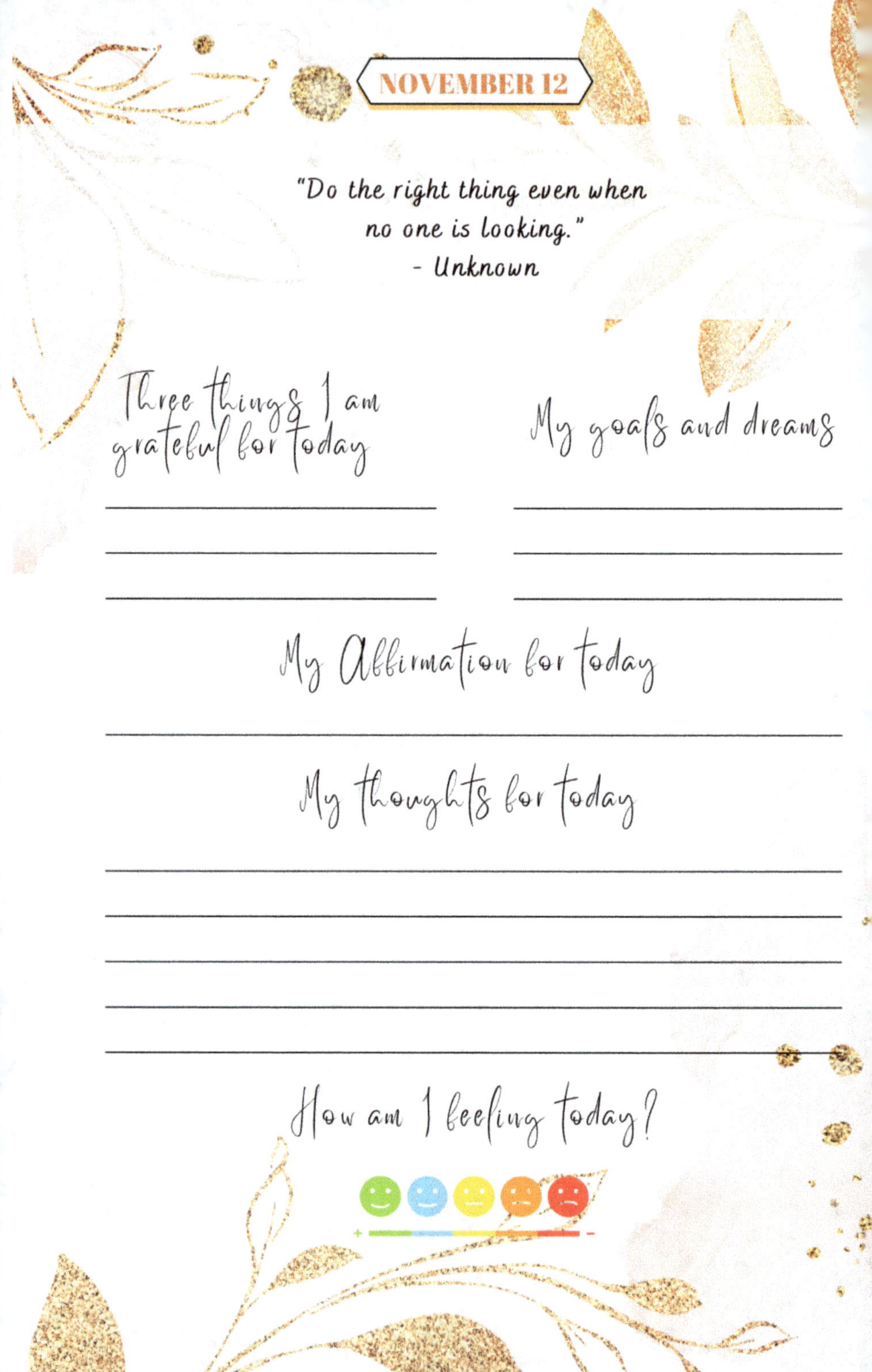

NOVEMBER 12

"Do the right thing even when no one is looking."
- Unknown

Three things I am grateful for today

My goals and dreams

My Affirmation for today

My thoughts for today

How am I feeling today?

+ –

"Wealth isn't about having a lot of money, it's about having a lot of options." - Chris Rock

Three things I am grateful for today

My goals and dreams

My Affirmation for today

My thoughts for today

How am I feeling today?

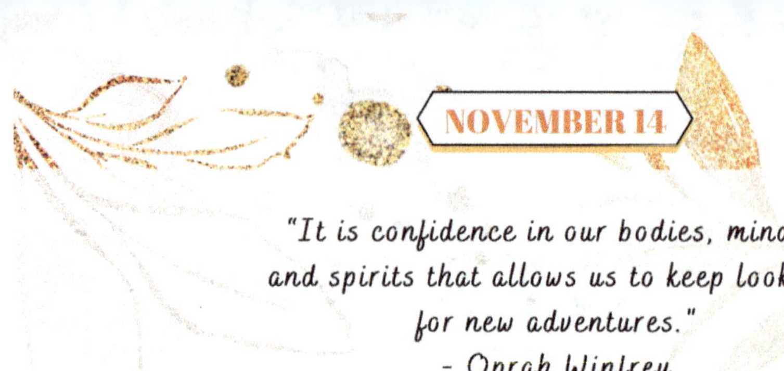

NOVEMBER 14

"It is confidence in our bodies, minds, and spirits that allows us to keep looking for new adventures."
- Oprah Winfrey

Three things I am grateful for today

___

___

___

My goals and dreams

___

___

___

My Affirmation for today

___

My thoughts for today

___

___

___

___

___

How am I feeling today?

NOVEMBER 15

"You were born to win, but to be a winner, you must plan to win, prepare to win, and expect to win."
- Zig Ziglar

Three things I am grateful for today

My goals and dreams

My Affirmation for today

My thoughts for today

How am I feeling today?

"There may be people that have more talent than you, but there's no excuse for anyone to work harder than you."
- Derek Jeter

Three things I am grateful for today

____

____

____

My goals and dreams

____

____

____

My Affirmation for today

____

My thoughts for today

____

____

____

____

____

How am I feeling today?

"If you judge people, you have
no time to love them."
- Mother Teresa

Three things I am grateful for today

My goals and dreams

My Affirmation for today

My thoughts for today

How am I feeling today?

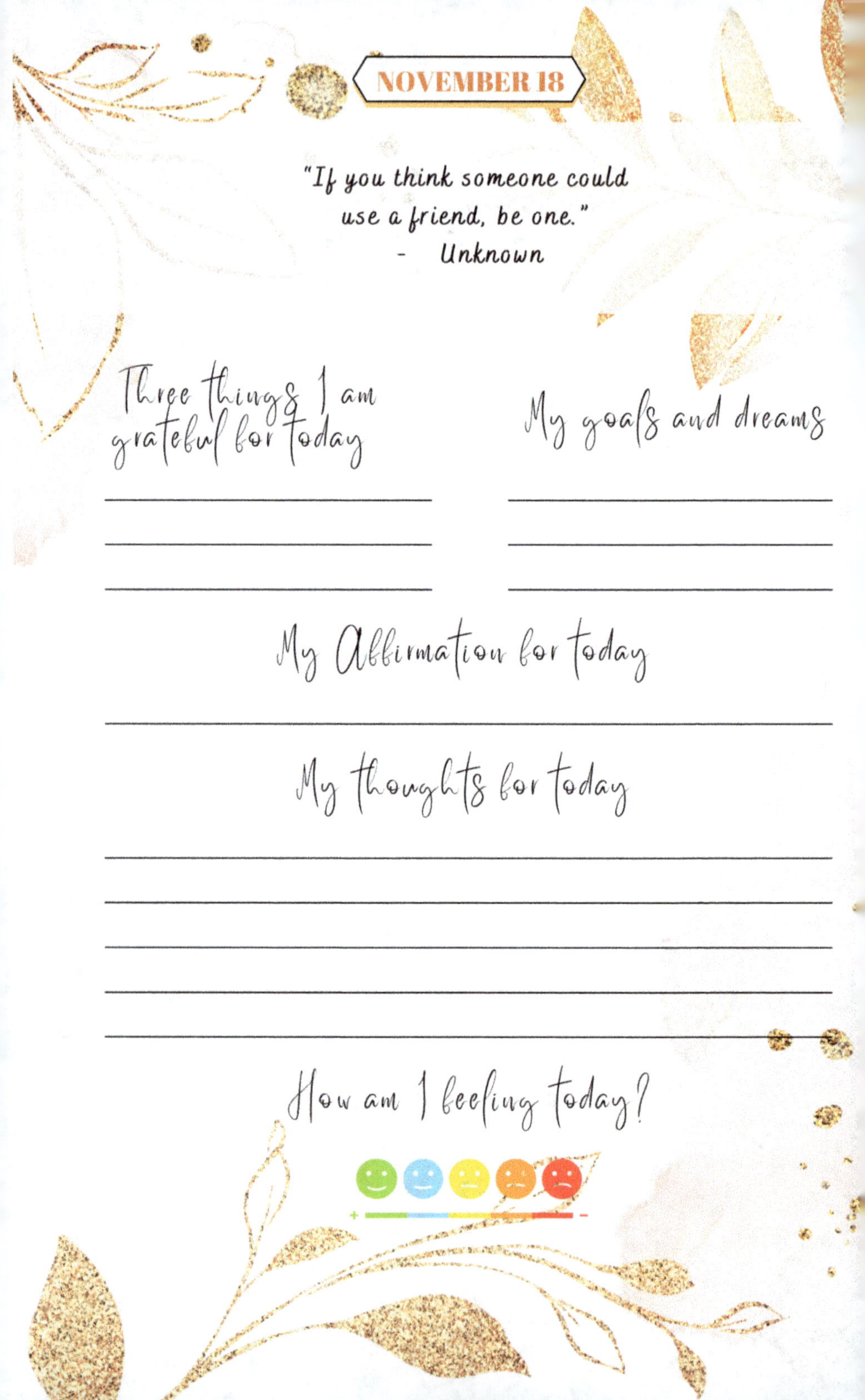

NOVEMBER 18

"If you think someone could use a friend, be one."
- Unknown

Three things I am grateful for today

My goals and dreams

My Affirmation for today

My thoughts for today

How am I feeling today?

NOVEMBER 19

"The woman who follows the crowd will usually
go no further than the crowd.
The woman who walks alone
is likely to find herself in places no one
has been before." - Albert Einstein

Three things I am grateful for today

My goals and dreams

My Affirmation for today

My thoughts for today

How am I feeling today?

NOVEMBER 20

"Do your little bit of good where you are;
it's those little bits of good put together
that overwhelm the world."
- Desmond Tutu

Three things I am grateful for today

My goals and dreams

My Affirmation for today

My thoughts for today

How am I feeling today?

"Courage isn't having the strength to go on—it is going on when you don't have strength." - Napoleon Bonaparte

Three things I am grateful for today

My goals and dreams

My Affirmation for today

My thoughts for today

How am I feeling today?

NOVEMBER 22

"My wish for you is that you continue. Continue to be who and how you are, to astonish a mean world with your acts of kindness. Continue to allow humor to lighten the burden of your tender heart." - Maya Angelou

Three things I am grateful for today

___
___
___

My goals and dreams

___
___
___

My Affirmation for today

___

My thoughts for today

___
___
___
___
___

How am I feeling today?

"How strongly you believe you really can will play the biggest part in determining if you actually will." - Lorri Faye

Three things I am grateful for today

My goals and dreams

My Affirmation for today

My thoughts for today

How am I feeling today?

"It's not what happens to you but how you react to it that matters." - Epictetus

Three things I am grateful for today

My goals and dreams

My Affirmation for today

My thoughts for today

How am I feeling today?

"Kindness and politeness are not overrated at all.
They're underused." - Tommy Lee Jones

Three things I am grateful for today

My goals and dreams

My Affirmation for today

My thoughts for today

How am I feeling today?

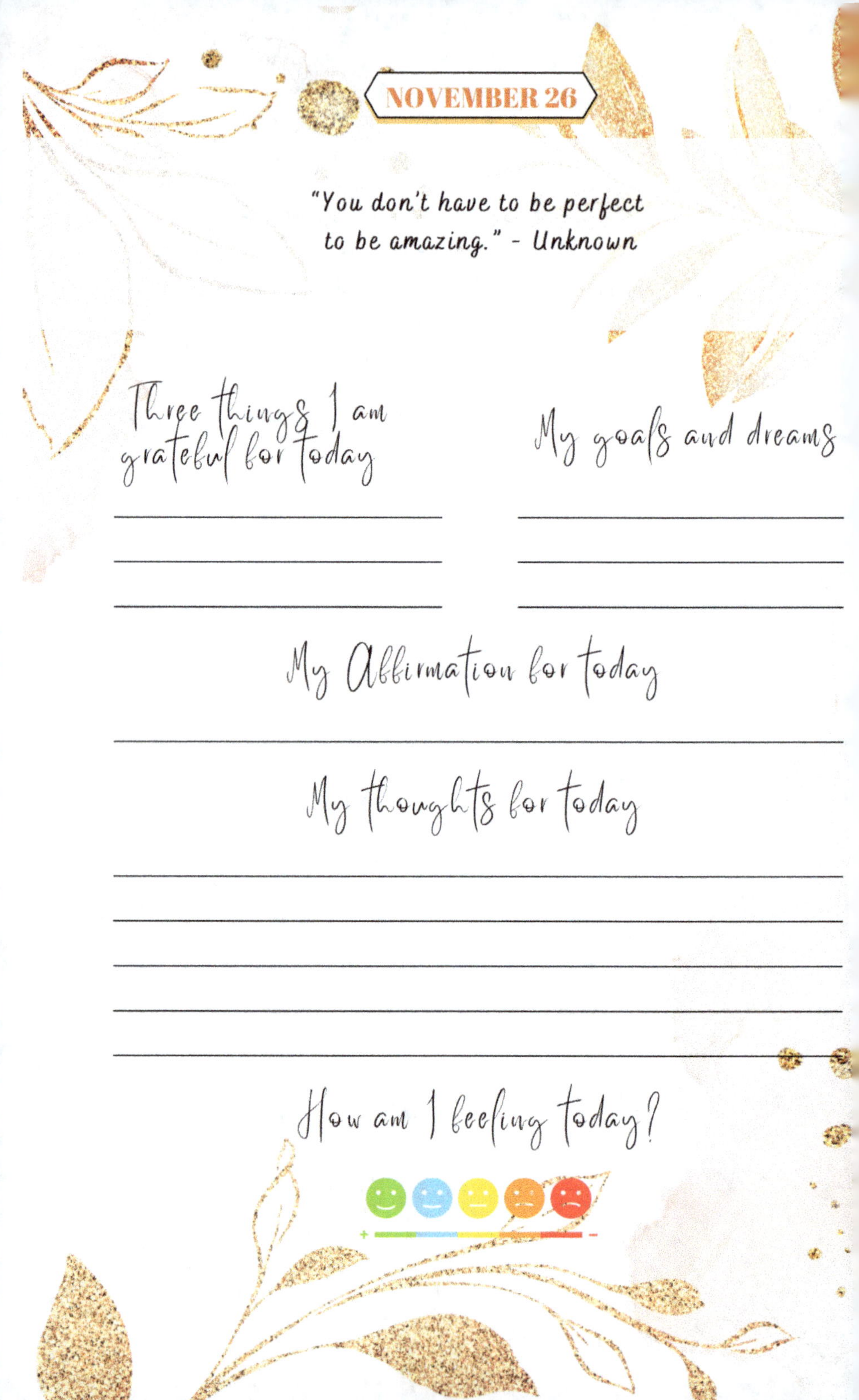

NOVEMBER 26

"You don't have to be perfect to be amazing." - Unknown

Three things I am grateful for today

My goals and dreams

My Affirmation for today

My thoughts for today

How am I feeling today?

NOVEMBER 27

"You can control two things: your work
ethic and your attitude
about anything." - Audre Lorde

Three things I am grateful for today

___

___

___

My goals and dreams

___

___

___

My Affirmation for today

___

My thoughts for today

___

___

___

___

___

How am I feeling today?

NOVEMBER 28

"You don't get paid for the hour. You get paid for the value you bring to the hour." - Jim Rohn

Three things I am grateful for today

My goals and dreams

My Affirmation for today

My thoughts for today

How am I feeling today?

"Courage is the greatest of all virtues because if you haven't courage, you may not have an opportunity to use any of the others." - Samuel Johnson

Three things I am grateful for today

____

____

____

My goals and dreams

____

____

____

My Affirmation for today

____

My thoughts for today

____

____

____

____

____

How am I feeling today?

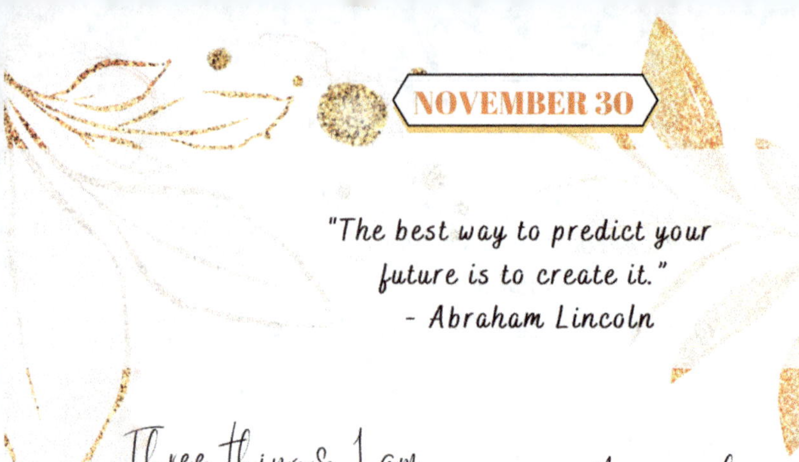

NOVEMBER 30

"The best way to predict your future is to create it."
- Abraham Lincoln

Three things I am grateful for today

My goals and dreams

My Affirmation for today

My thoughts for today

How am I feeling today?

DECEMBER 1

"A goal is a dream with a deadline."
- Napoleon Hill

Three things I am grateful for

____

____

____

My goals and dreams

____

____

____

My Affirmation for today

____

My thoughts for today

____

____

____

____

____

How am I feeling today?

\+ –

DECEMBER 2

"A successful man is one who can lay a firm foundation with the bricks others have thrown at him." - David Brinkley

Three things I am grateful for

____

____

____

My goals and dreams

____

____

____

My Affirmation for today

____

My thoughts for today

____

____

____

____

____

How am I feeling today?

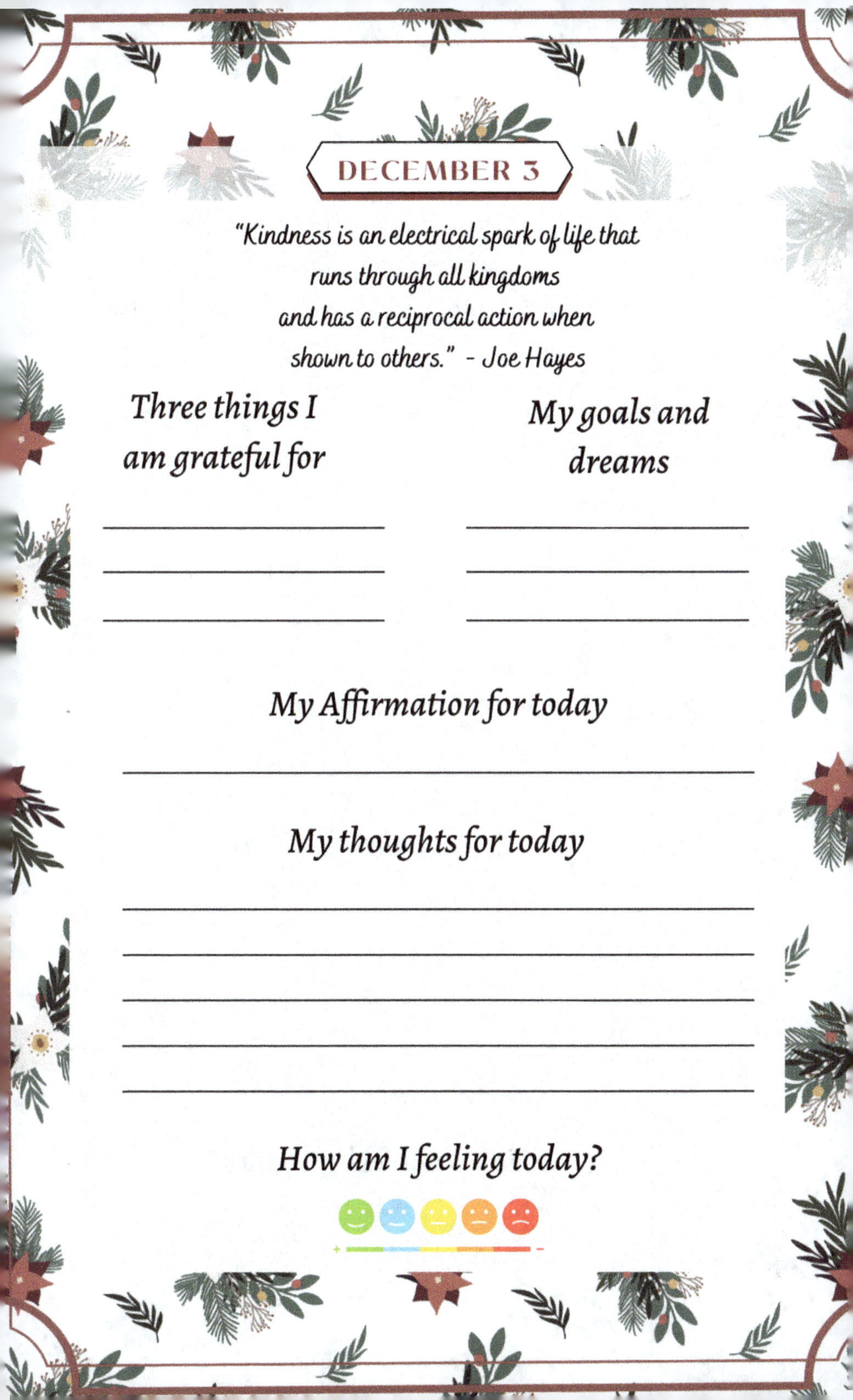

DECEMBER 3

"Kindness is an electrical spark of life that runs through all kingdoms and has a reciprocal action when shown to others." - Joe Hayes

Three things I am grateful for

My goals and dreams

My Affirmation for today

My thoughts for today

How am I feeling today?

DECEMBER 4

"We gain strength, courage and confidence by each experience in which we really stop to look fear in the face." - Eleanor Roosevelt

Three things I am grateful for

My goals and dreams

My Affirmation for today

My thoughts for today

How am I feeling today?

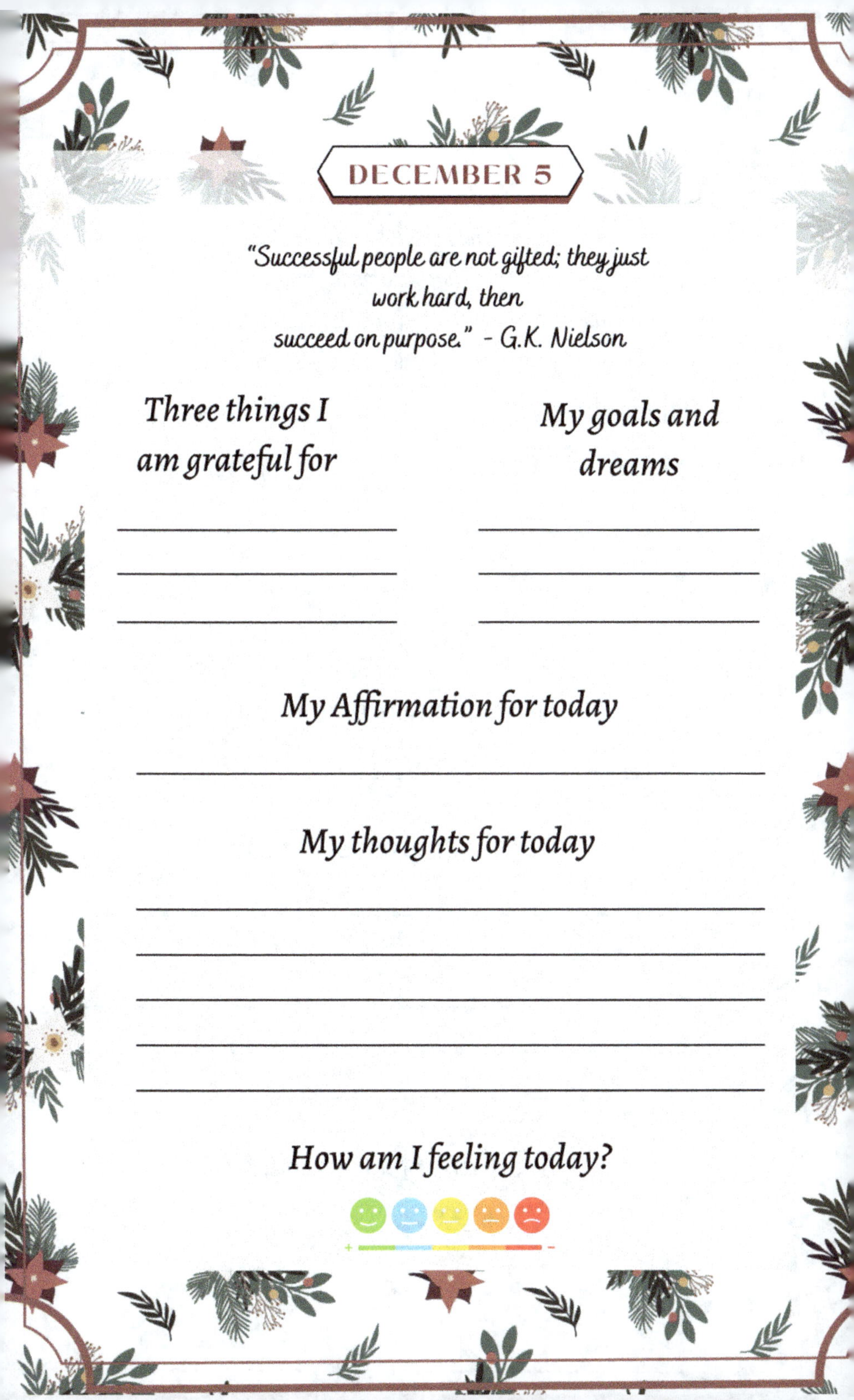

DECEMBER 5

"Successful people are not gifted; they just work hard, then succeed on purpose." - G.K. Nielson

Three things I am grateful for

___

___

___

My goals and dreams

___

___

___

My Affirmation for today

___

My thoughts for today

___

___

___

___

___

How am I feeling today?

DECEMBER 6

*"Gratitude helps you to grow and expand;
gratitude brings joy and
laughter into your life and into the lives of all
those around you." - Eileen Caddy*

Three things I am grateful for

___

___

___

My goals and dreams

___

___

___

My Affirmation for today

___

My thoughts for today

___

___

___

___

___

How am I feeling today?

+ –

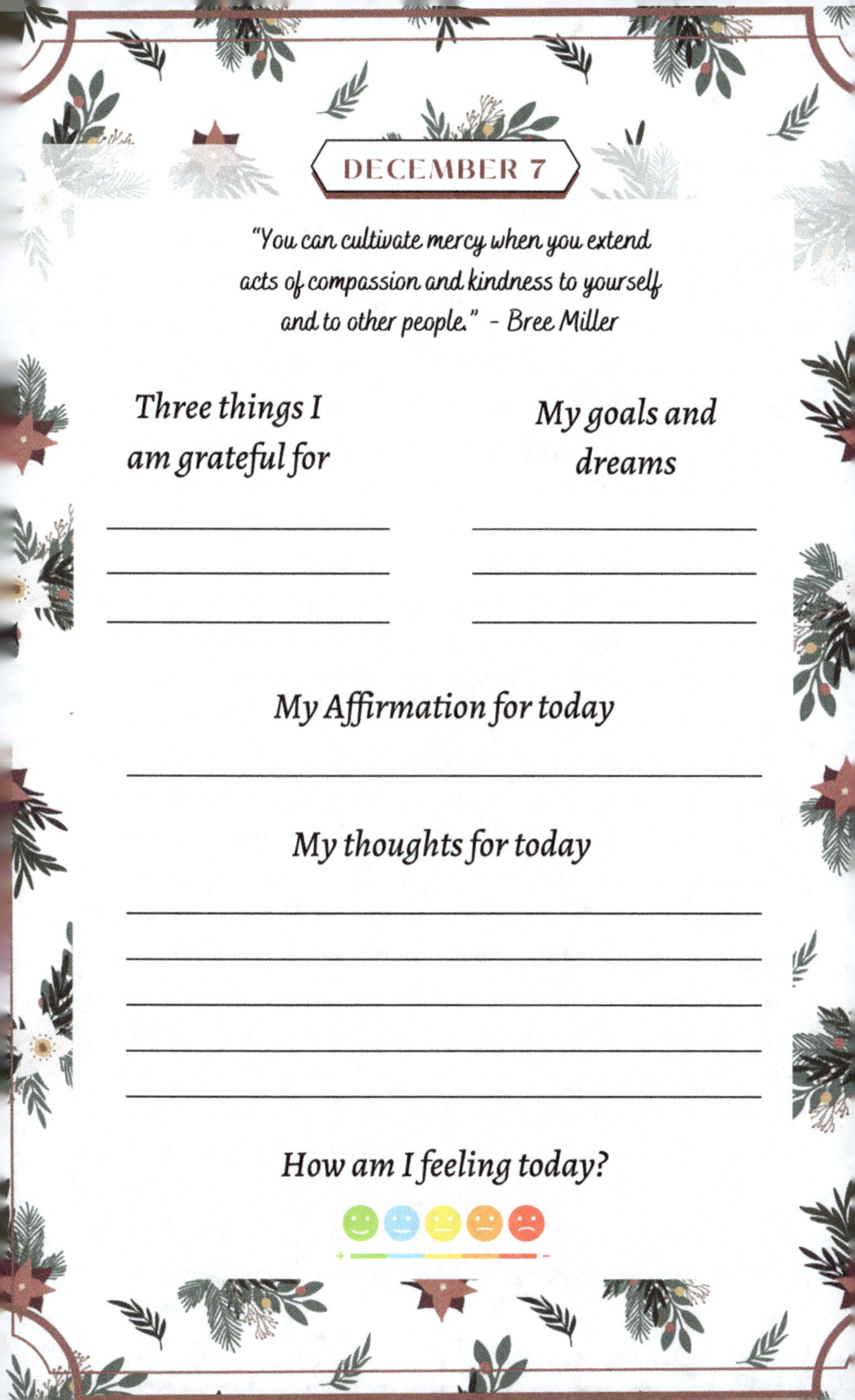

DECEMBER 7

"You can cultivate mercy when you extend acts of compassion and kindness to yourself and to other people." - Bree Miller

Three things I am grateful for

My goals and dreams

My Affirmation for today

My thoughts for today

How am I feeling today?

DECEMBER 8

"Life is 10% what happens to you and 90% how you react to it."
- Charles R. Swindoll

Three things I am grateful for

____
____
____

My goals and dreams

____
____
____

My Affirmation for today

____

My thoughts for today

____
____
____
____
____

How am I feeling today?

DECEMBER 9

"It is the characteristic of the magnanimous man to ask no favor but to be ready to do kindness to others." - Aristotle

Three things I am grateful for

My goals and dreams

My Affirmation for today

My thoughts for today

How am I feeling today?

DECEMBER 10

"Sooner or later, those who win are those who think they can." - Paul Tournier

Three things I am grateful for

My goals and dreams

My Affirmation for today

My thoughts for today

How am I feeling today?

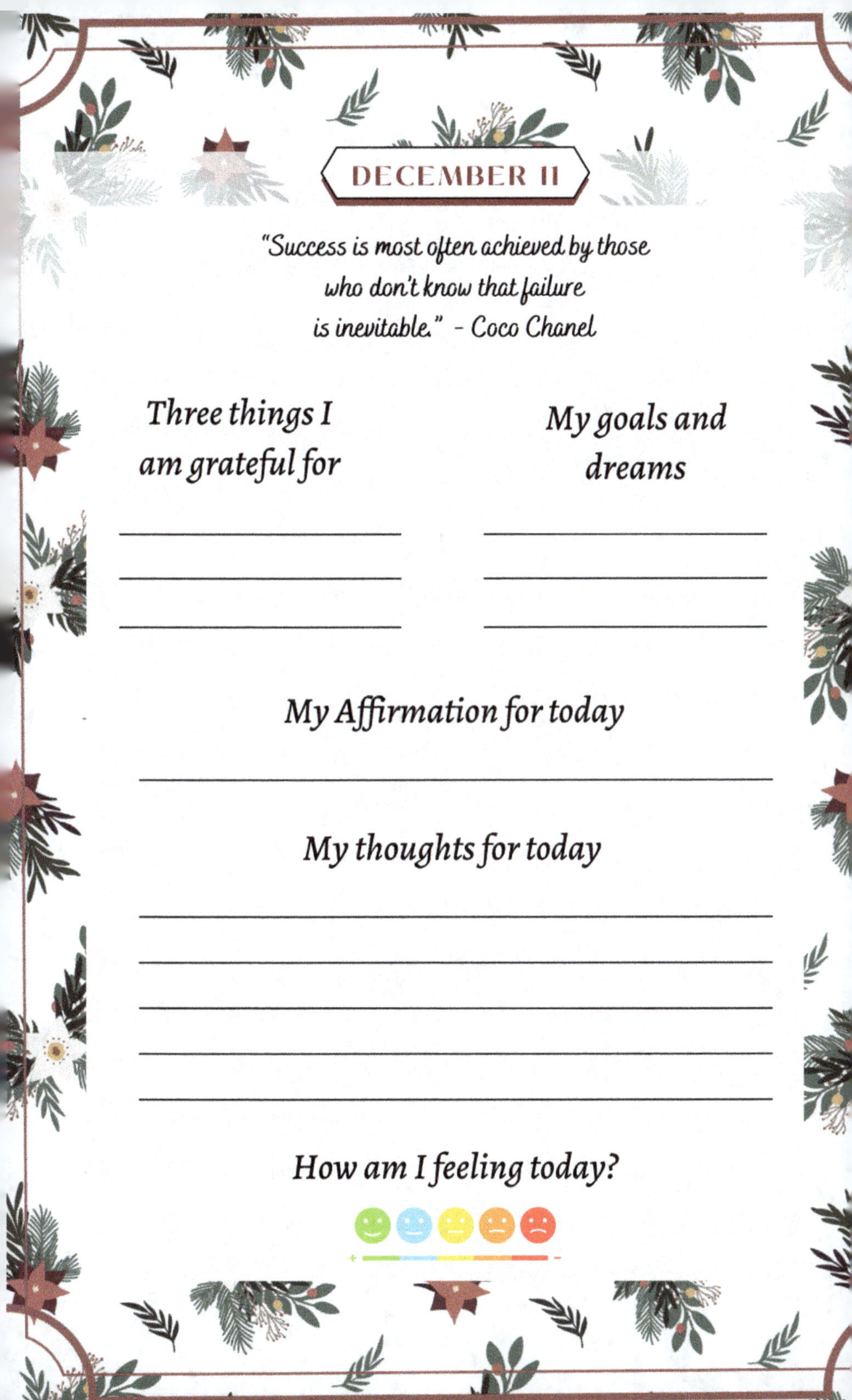

DECEMBER 11

"Success is most often achieved by those who don't know that failure is inevitable." - Coco Chanel

Three things I am grateful for

My goals and dreams

My Affirmation for today

My thoughts for today

How am I feeling today?

DECEMBER 12

"A diamond is merely a lump of coal that did well under pressure." - Unknown

Three things I am grateful for

My goals and dreams

My Affirmation for today

My thoughts for today

How am I feeling today?

DECEMBER 13

"When I win and when I lose, I take ownership of it, because I really am in charge of what I do." - Nicki Minaj

Three things I am grateful for

My goals and dreams

My Affirmation for today

My thoughts for today

How am I feeling today?

+ –

DECEMBER 14

"The two most important days in your life
are the day you're born
and the day you find out why." - Mark Twain

Three things I am grateful for

____

____

____

My goals and dreams

____

____

____

My Affirmation for today

____

My thoughts for today

____

____

____

____

____

How am I feeling today?

DECEMBER 15

"You can accomplish by kindness what you cannot by force."
- Publilius Syrus

Three things I am grateful for

My goals and dreams

My Affirmation for today

My thoughts for today

How am I feeling today?

DECEMBER 16

"Nothing ever goes away until it teaches us what we need to know." - Pema Chodron

Three things I am grateful for

___

___

___

My goals and dreams

___

___

___

My Affirmation for today

___

My thoughts for today

___

___

___

___

___

How am I feeling today?

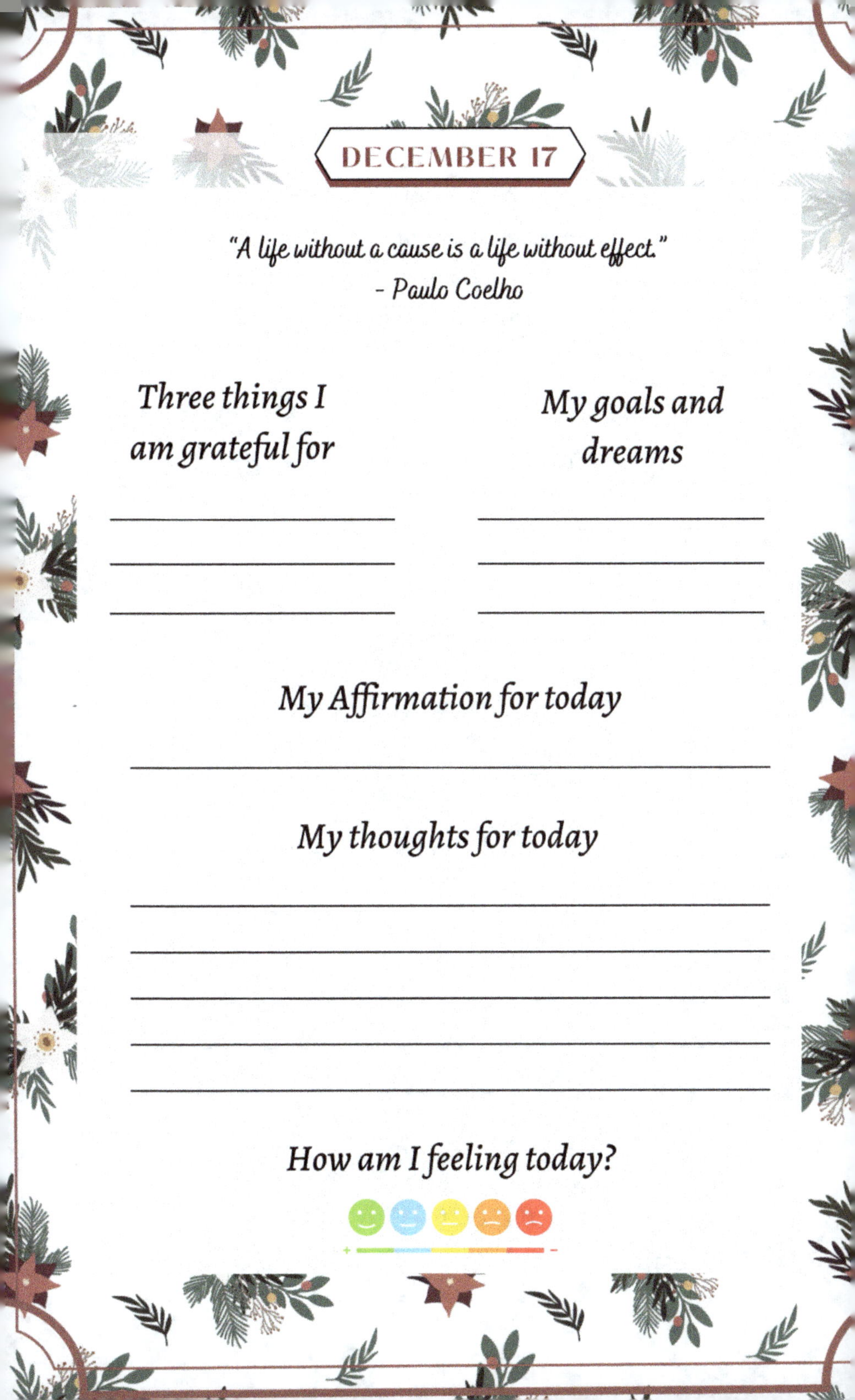

DECEMBER 17

"A life without a cause is a life without effect."
- Paulo Coelho

Three things I am grateful for

My goals and dreams

My Affirmation for today

My thoughts for today

How am I feeling today?

DECEMBER 18

"Confidence is everything. Confidence is what makes that simple white tee and jeans look good." - Ciara

Three things I am grateful for

My goals and dreams

My Affirmation for today

My thoughts for today

How am I feeling today?

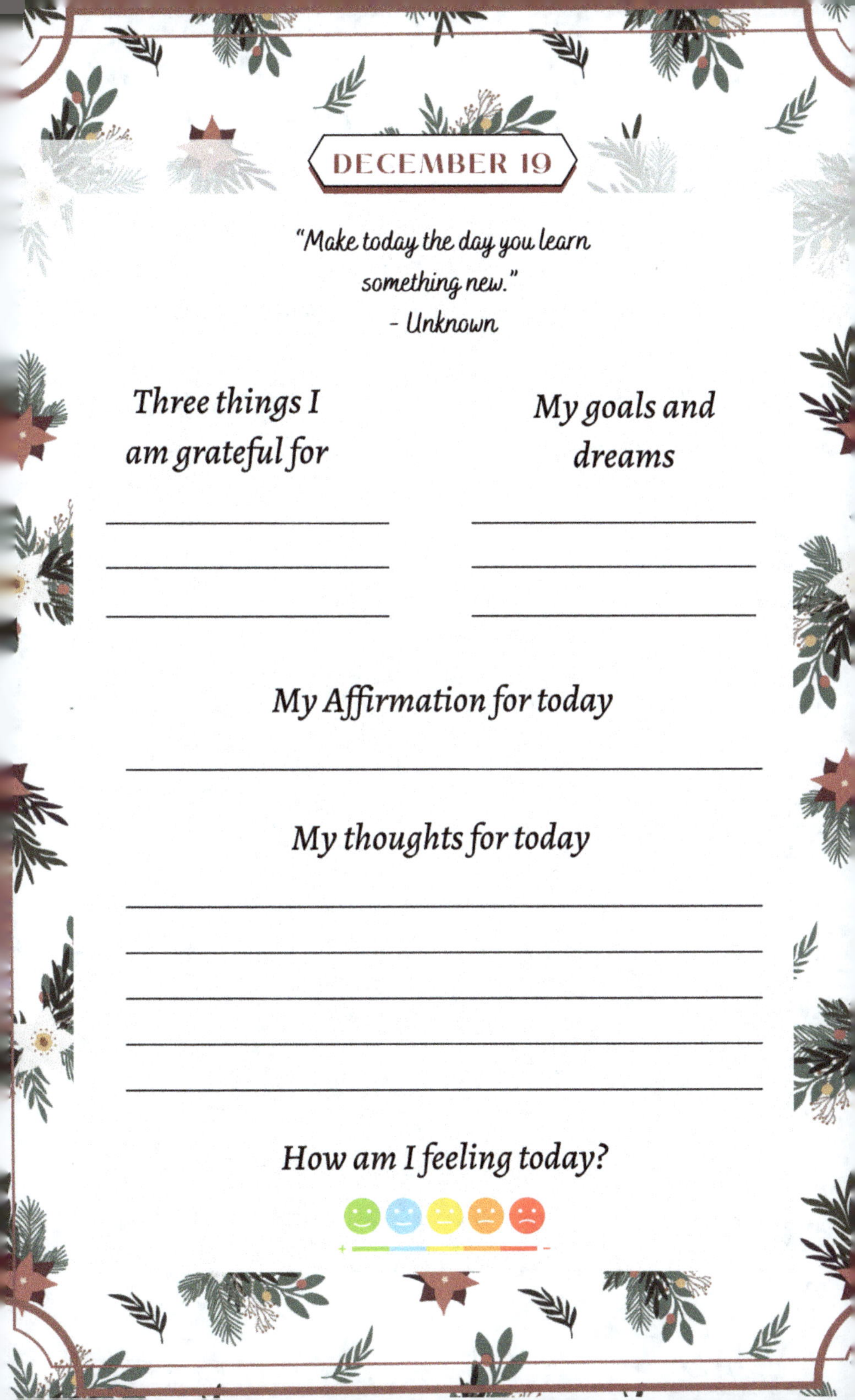

DECEMBER 19

"Make today the day you learn something new."
- Unknown

Three things I am grateful for

My goals and dreams

My Affirmation for today

My thoughts for today

How am I feeling today?

"Do things for people not because of who they are or what they do in return, but because of who you are." - Harold S. Kushner

Three things I am grateful for

____

____

____

My goals and dreams

____

____

____

My Affirmation for today

____

My thoughts for today

____

____

____

____

____

How am I feeling today?

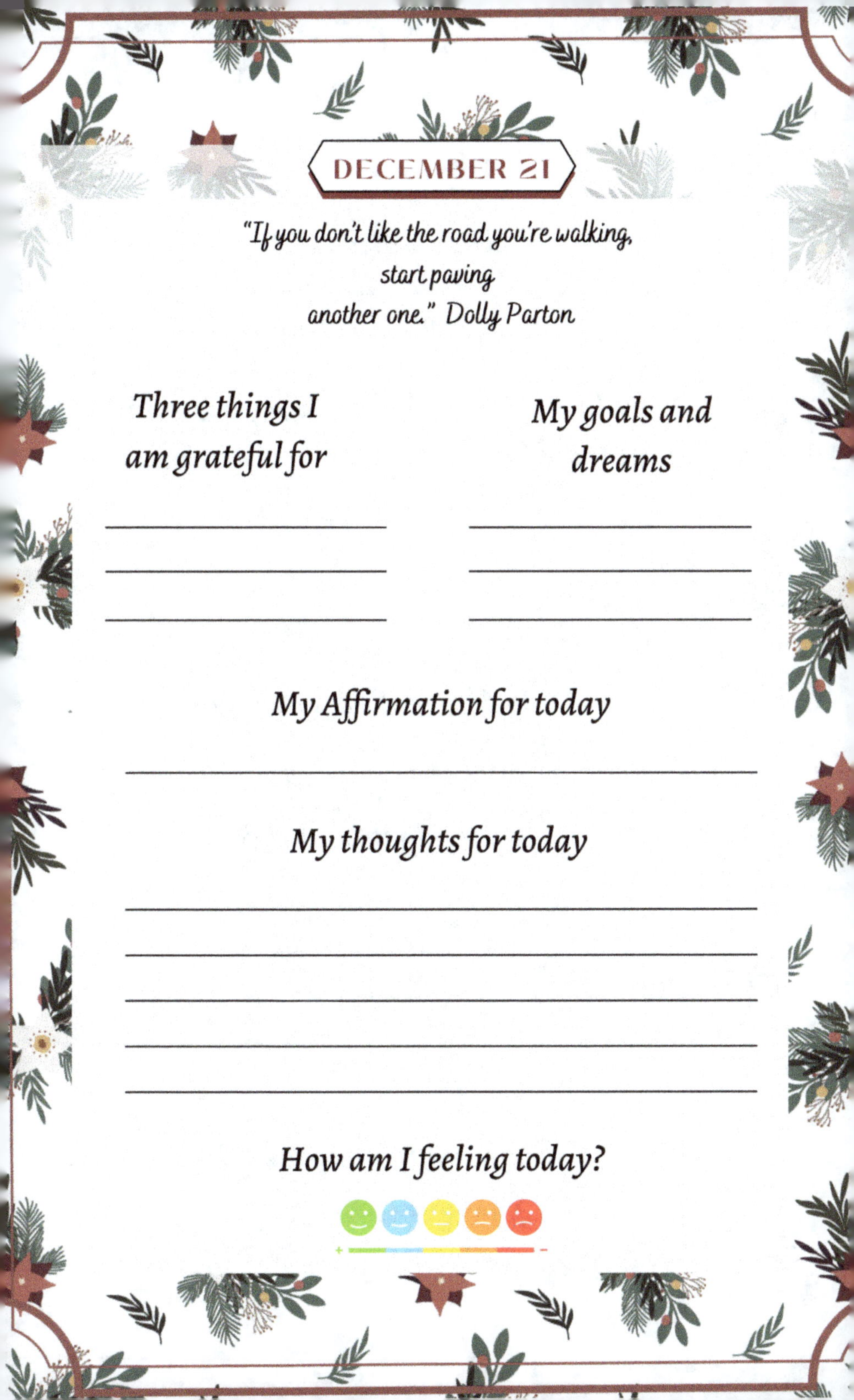

DECEMBER 21

"If you don't like the road you're walking,
start paving
another one." Dolly Parton

Three things I am grateful for

My goals and dreams

My Affirmation for today

My thoughts for today

How am I feeling today?

DECEMBER 22

"In order to be irreplaceable, one must always be different." - Coco Chanel

Three things I am grateful for

My goals and dreams

My Affirmation for today

My thoughts for today

How am I feeling today?

DECEMBER 23

"If today you are a little bit better than you were yesterday, then that's enough." - David A. Bednar

Three things I am grateful for

My goals and dreams

My Affirmation for today

My thoughts for today

How am I feeling today?

DECEMBER 24

"Simple kindness may be the most vital key to the riddle of how human beings can live with each other in peace and care properly for this planet we all share." - Bo Lozoff

Three things I am grateful for

___

___

___

My goals and dreams

___

___

___

My Affirmation for today

___

My thoughts for today

___

___

___

___

___

How am I feeling today?

+ –

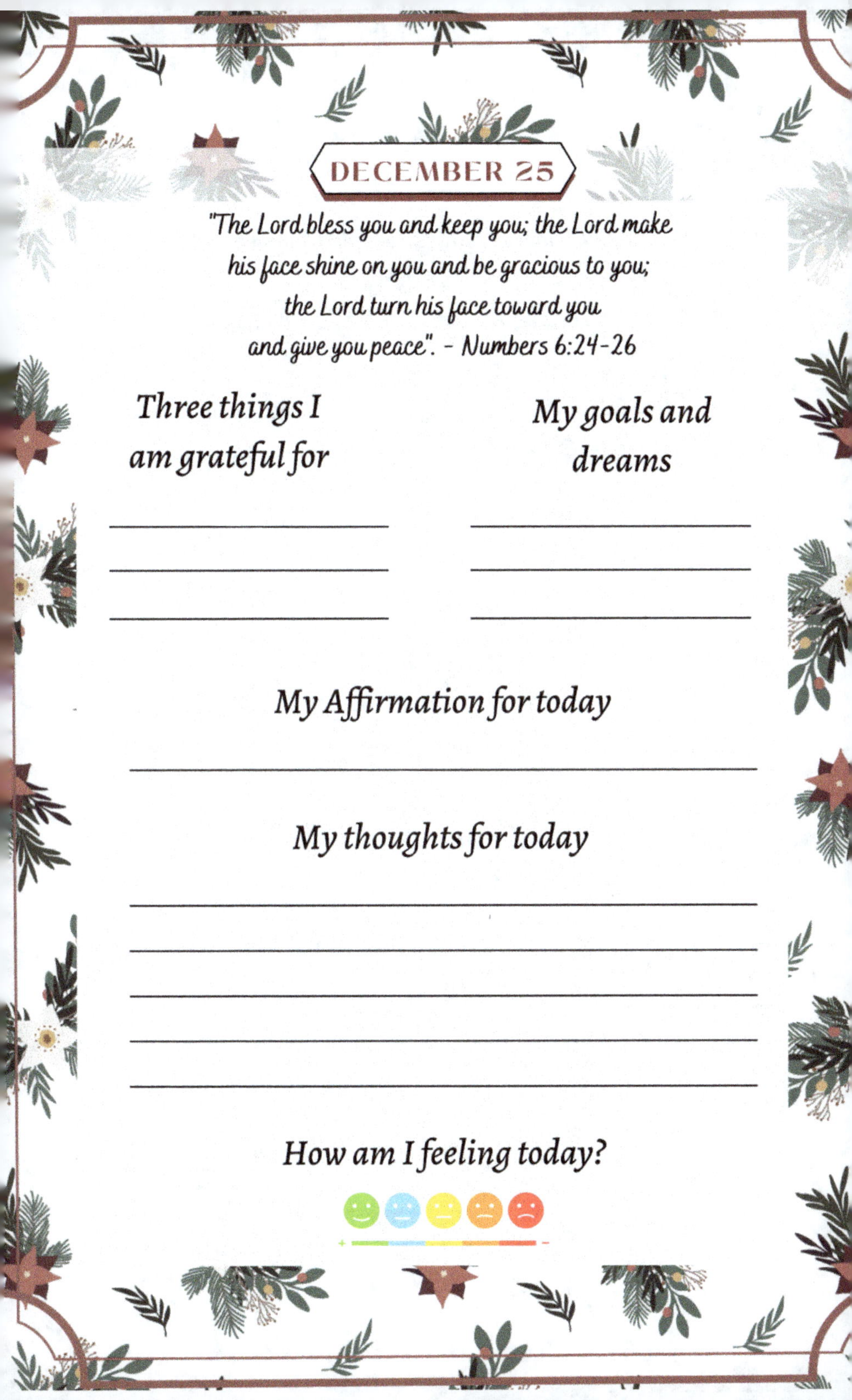

DECEMBER 25

"The Lord bless you and keep you; the Lord make his face shine on you and be gracious to you; the Lord turn his face toward you and give you peace". - Numbers 6:24-26

Three things I am grateful for

____

____

____

My goals and dreams

____

____

____

My Affirmation for today

____

My thoughts for today

____

____

____

____

____

How am I feeling today?

DECEMBER 26

"Change is painful, but nothing is as painful as staying stuck somewhere you don't belong." - Mandy Hale

Three things I am grateful for

My goals and dreams

My Affirmation for today

My thoughts for today

How am I feeling today?

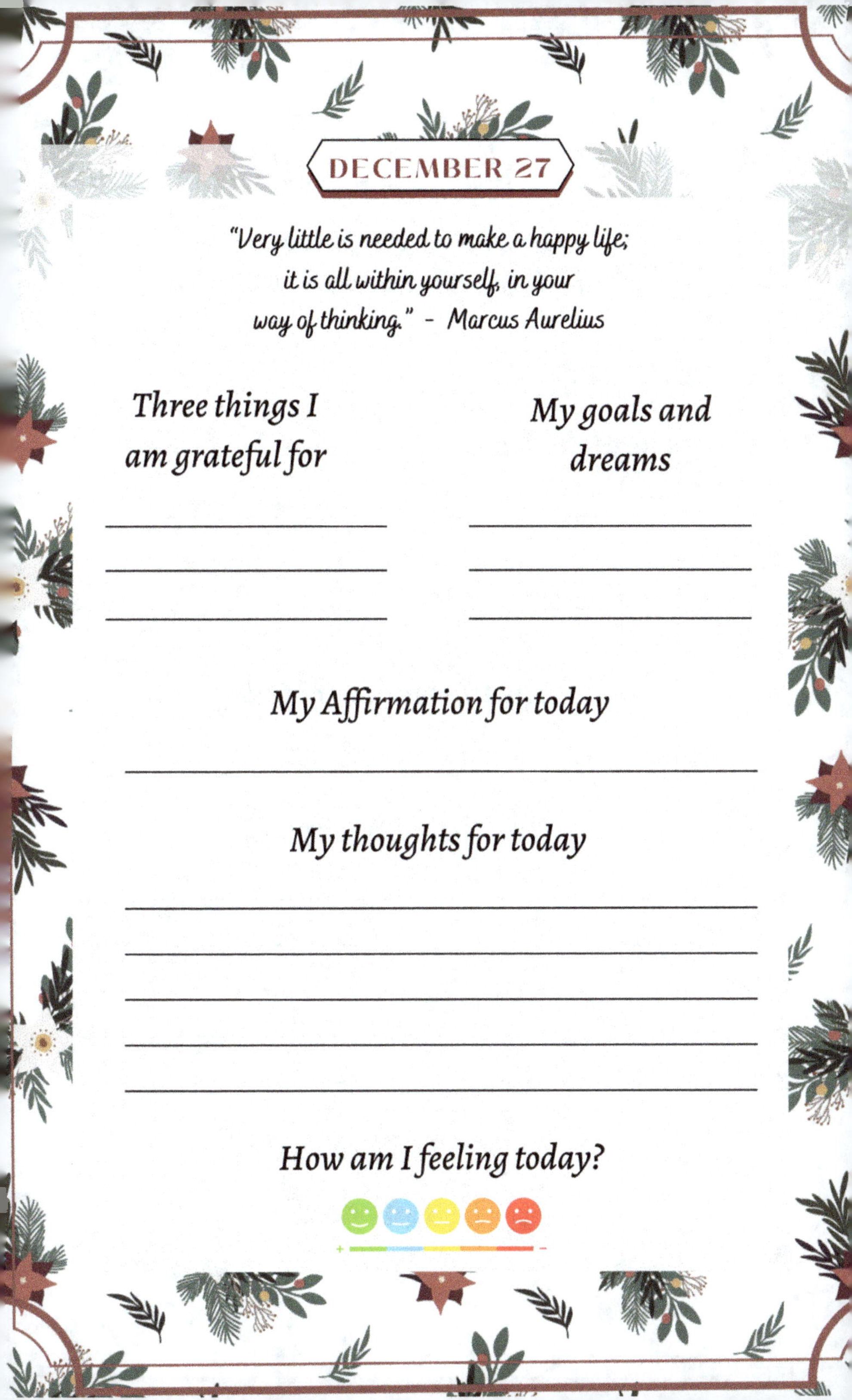

DECEMBER 27

"Very little is needed to make a happy life; it is all within yourself, in your way of thinking." - Marcus Aurelius

Three things I am grateful for

___

___

___

My goals and dreams

___

___

___

My Affirmation for today

___

My thoughts for today

___

___

___

___

___

How am I feeling today?

+ –

DECEMBER 28

"Life's like a movie; write your own ending.
Keep believing, keep pretending" - Jim Henson

Three things I am grateful for

My goals and dreams

My Affirmation for today

My thoughts for today

How am I feeling today?

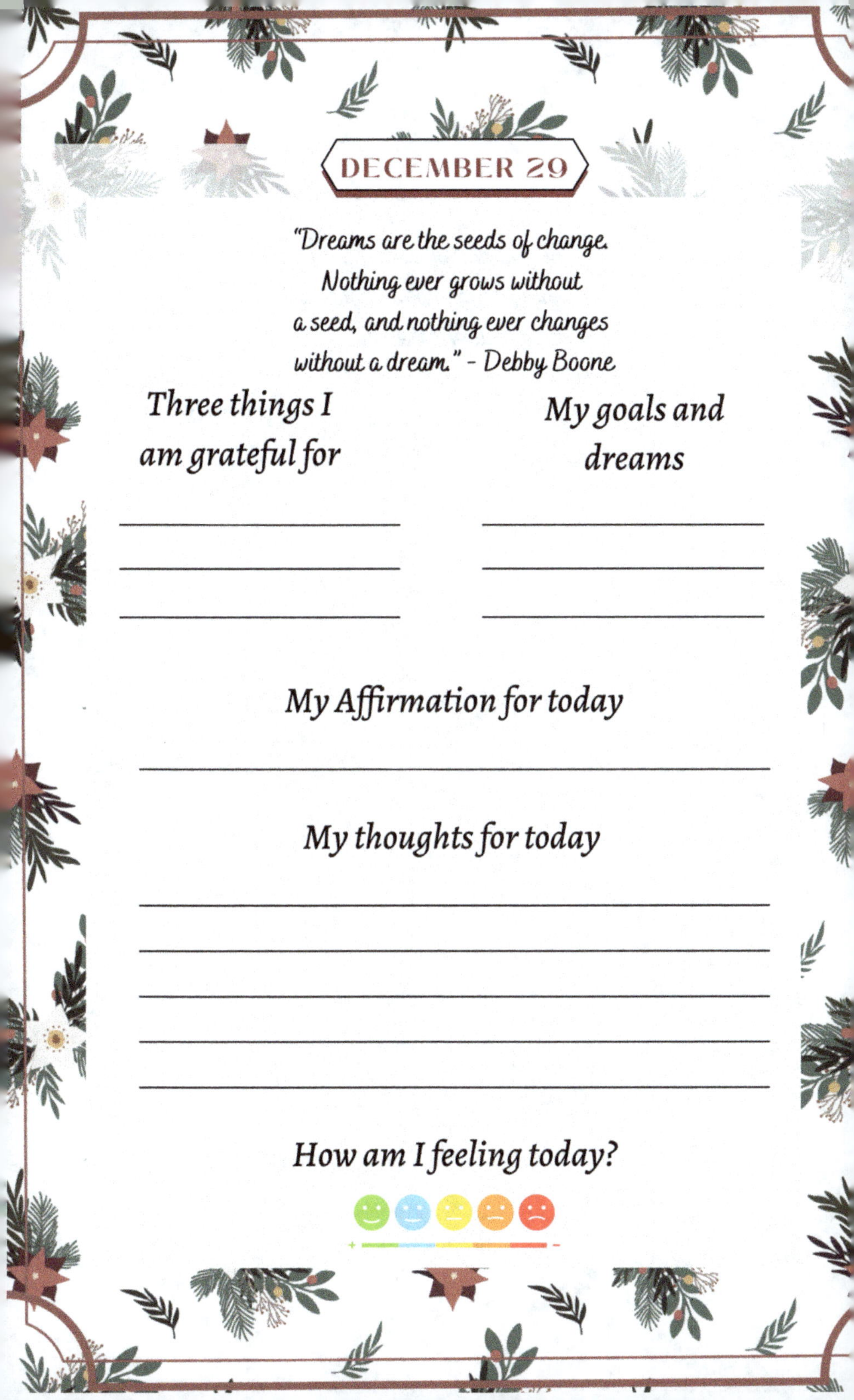

DECEMBER 29

"Dreams are the seeds of change. Nothing ever grows without a seed, and nothing ever changes without a dream." - Debby Boone

Three things I am grateful for

My goals and dreams

My Affirmation for today

My thoughts for today

How am I feeling today?

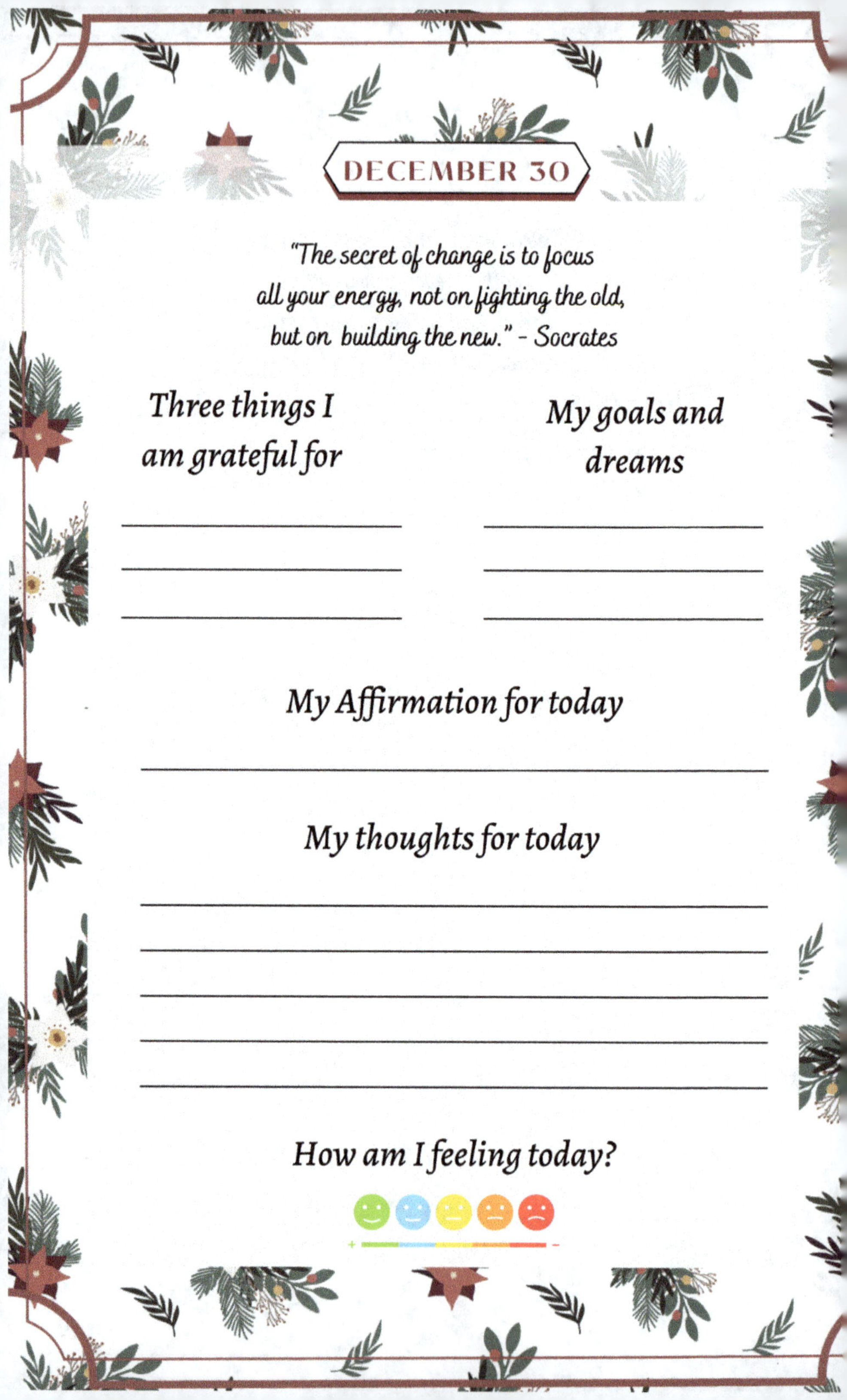

DECEMBER 30

"The secret of change is to focus all your energy, not on fighting the old, but on building the new." - Socrates

Three things I am grateful for

My goals and dreams

My Affirmation for today

My thoughts for today

How am I feeling today?

DECEMBER 31

"What is coming is better than what is gone." - Unknown

Three things I am grateful for

My goals and dreams

My Affirmation for today

My thoughts for today

How am I feeling today?

www.ingramcontent.com/pod-product-compliance
Lightning Source LLC
Chambersburg PA
CBHW061058210726
48294CB00001B/204

* 9 7 8 1 7 3 9 6 2 0 8 3 7 *